GET THINGS DONE

The Action Taker's Guide to Overcoming Excuses

BY

Richard B. Monger

- **Chapter 1 The Power of Action-Taking Mindset**

Unveiling the mindset that separates Action Takers from the rest.

How to shift your perspective and embrace a proactive approach.

The psychology of motivation: Igniting the fire within to drive action.

- **Chapter 2 Breaking the Chains of Procrastination**

Understanding the science behind procrastination and its impact.

Proven techniques to overcome the urge to delay tasks.

Cultivating discipline and building a consistent work ethic.

- **Chapter 3 From Excuses to Execution: Your Action Plan**

Crafting a concrete action plan that bridges the gap between ideas and execution.

Goal setting techniques that compel you to take immediate steps.

How to track progress and stay accountable to yourself.

- **Chapter 4 Embracing Challenges and Overcoming Setbacks**

Navigating roadblocks and setbacks with resilience and determination.

Turning failures into stepping stones toward success.

The art of adapting and thriving in the face of adversity.

- **Chapter 5 Time Mastery: Making Every Moment Count**

Strategies for optimizing your time and maximizing productivity.

Techniques to prioritize tasks and eliminate time-wasting activities.

Creating a balanced routine that fosters efficiency and well-being.

Identifying common distractions and their impact on your progress.

Mindfulness and concentration exercises to enhance focus.

Designing an environment that supports your undivided attention.

Understanding the science of habit formation and its role in success.

How to replace old habits with productive action-taking routines.

Nurturing habits that become second nature and drive consistent results.

Strategies for maintaining momentum and avoiding complacency.

Creating a legacy of action and inspiring others through your journey.

Conclusion

Introduction

In a world filled with dreams, ideas, and ambitions, the line between those who merely imagine and those who truly achieve is drawn by one defining trait: the ability to take action. Welcome to a journey that will enable you to step bravely onto the path of the Action Taker, where excuses are broken, and goals are achieved.

In the following pages, we will start on a changing study of what sets the doers apart from the thinkers. This book is not just about motivation or inspiration—it's a practical guide that will give you with the tools, strategies, and mindset needed to move yourself from the realm of purpose to the realm of accomplishment.

Chapter by chapter, we will examine the complex components that add to the art of successful action taking. From understanding the psychology behind delay to mastering time management, from accepting challenges as opportunities to developing action-oriented habits, we will dig deep into the principles that drive success.

But this isn't just a solo trip. You'll discover the deep impact of responsibility and support, as well as the changing nature of beating fear and accepting growth. Each lesson learned and skill gained will make a new link in the chain that pushes you forward, closer to your goals.

Are you ready to leave behind the circle of excuses and start on a life marked by success, satisfaction, and progress? The parts that follow will serve as your guide. Consider this book your partner as you travel the terrain of action-taking, pushing yourself toward a future filled with successes.

So, turn the page and step onto the path of the Action Taker. Let's eliminate excuses, break barriers, and spark the flame of constant, purposeful action. Your journey starts now.

Chapter 1
The Power of Action-Taking Mindset

Welcome to the first part of our exciting trip together in "Get Things Done: The Action Taker's Guide to Overcoming Excuses"! In this chapter, we're going deep into the magical world of the Action-Taking Mindset, where the seeds of success are sown and dreams are turned into reality.

Picture this: you're standing at the edge of a huge ocean of possibilities, and the only thing holding you back is your attitude. But fear not, because we're about to give you with the tools and knowledge you need to release the power within you.

Embrace the Attitude of Possibility
We kick things off by debunking the idea that some people are just born with an action-taking attitude while others aren't. We'll show how the attitude of potential is within your reach and how you can start developing it today. Remember, every big achievement started with a single thought.

Rewiring Your Brain for Success

Did you know your brain is like a machine, capable of rewriting itself for success? We'll take you through the science behind neuroplasticity and show you how small, consistent actions can lead to big changes in your thought processes. Get ready to change your mind for action!

The Ripple Effect of Positive Thinking

Positive thought isn't just a fluffy idea; it's a game-changer. We'll study how your thoughts affect your deeds and the world around you. From the "glass half full" viewpoint to the power of mantras, you'll learn how to harness the ripple effect of positive thought.

Embracing Failures as Stepping Stones

No action-taking trip is complete without a few bumps along the way. We'll dive into the art of accepting mistakes as chances for growth. Learn how to view failures as stepping stones that push you closer to your goals, and turn challenges into useful lessons.

The Momentum of Action
Ever noticed how taking that first step seems to make everything else fall into place? We'll discover the secret behind the energy of action and how even the smallest actions can create a snowball effect that pushes you forward. Get ready to experience the thrilling rush of progress!

Cultivating a Can-Do Attitude
Imagine having an inner fan who believes in you no matter what. That's the power of a can-do attitude, and we'll show you how to develop it. We'll share useful methods to quiet your inner critic and replace it with a helpful and encouraging voice.

Shifting from Overthinking to Doing Analysis paralysis, anyone? We've all been there, but don't worry, we've got your back. Discover how to change from overthinking mode to action mode. You'll learn techniques to quiet the endless loops of doubt and finally start putting your bright ideas into motion.

The Choice to Take Action
At the heart of the action-taking mindset lies a simple yet deep choice: to take action or not. We'll help you through the process of making conscious

Choices that match with your goals. By the end of this chapter, you'll be equipped with the power to choose action every time.

Your Action-Taking Mantra

As you start on this amazing trip, we'll help you create your very own action-taking mantra—a phrase that sparks your drive and pushes you into action. Get ready to fill your days with fresh energy and excitement!

A Community of Action Takers

Before we wrap up, we invite you to join our group of fellow Action Takers. Share your thoughts, progress, and problems as we help each other on this exciting road to success. Together, we're unbeatable!

Get ready to unlock the full potential of your action-taking attitude. Remember, every step you take brings you closer to the life you imagine. So, let's dive into the rest of this book and start accepting the power of action like never before. Your journey starts here, and the options are endless!

Unveiling the Mindset that Sets Action Takers Apart

Have you ever thought what separates those who regularly take action and achieve their goals from those who find themselves stuck in a circle of inaction and lost opportunities? The secret lies in the attitude – the way we think, assess obstacles, and approach jobs. In this chapter, we're digging deep into the attitude that empowers Action Takers, giving you with useful insights and simple methods to adopt in your own life.

Embrace the "Start Small" Mentality:

Action Takers understand that every big achievement starts with a small step. They don't wait for the right time; they start with what they have, where they are. It's like making a puzzle – one piece at a time finally makes the whole picture. Begin with a doable job, and as you conquer each step, you'll gain the energy to face more important tasks.

See Failure as Feedback, Not Defeat:

Action Takers view loss as a stepping stone, not a tripping block. They understand that failures offer important lessons that help to growth. Instead of being disheartened by a failure, they examine it, learn from it, and change their approach. By viewing failure as feedback, you can lessen the fear that often holds us back and move forward with renewed drive.

Focus on Progress, Not Perfection:

Perfectionism can be a big roadblock to taking action. Action Takers understand that perfection is a myth and that progress is what truly counts. By changing your focus from getting perfect results to making regular progress, you'll ease the pressure and worry that often stop us. Celebrate each step forward, no matter how small, and you'll stay inspired to keep going.

Embrace a "Can-Do" Attitude:

Your mood shapes your world. Action Takers keep a positive and upbeat attitude that drives their confidence to take on tasks. Replace self-doubt and negative self-talk with powerful mantras. Instead of

Saying, "I can't do this," shift to "I can figure this out." This simple change can have a deep effect on your desire to take action.

Visualize Success and Set Clear Intentions:

Before taking action, picture yourself succeeding. Imagine the good results and how it will feel to achieve your goals. This mental exercise not only boosts your confidence but also primes your brain for action. Combine this with setting clear goals – describe what you want to achieve and explain the steps to get there. This clarity serves as a guide, making it easier to take action.

Make Action a Habit:

Action Takers understand that discipline is key. They make taking action a habit by adding it into their daily tasks. Start small – commit to spending a particular time each day to work on your goals. Over time, this regularity will become second nature, and you'll find yourself easily pulled to taking action without overthinking it.

Embrace the Learning Process:

Instead of fearing the unknown, Action Takers welcome it. They view obstacles as chances to learn and grow. Approach jobs with a desire to find, learn, and improve. By viewing obstacles as chances to expand your skills and knowledge, you'll create an attitude that accepts action.

Remember, the attitude of an Action Taker is not a fixed trait – it's a skill that can be developed over time. Start by adding these simple strategies into your daily life, and watch as your desire to take action changes your goals from dreams into reality. The trip of a thousand miles starts with a single step, so take that step today and accept the attitude of an Action Taker!

Shifting Your Perspective: Embracing a Proactive Approach

Have you ever felt stuck, watching chances pass you by? It's time to break free from that circle and step into a new mindset—a attitude of aggressive action-taking. In this chapter, we'll study the art of changing your viewpoint and taking a strategic approach to life. Get ready to start on a journey that will inspire you to take charge, make things happen, and build the life you truly desire.

The Power of Perspective:
Picture this: You wake up to a new day, and instead of waiting for things to happen, you decide to make things happen. That's the heart of a responsible attitude. It's about viewing life as a surface on which you hold the brush, ready to paint your own creation. By changing your viewpoint, you'll stop being a silent watcher and become the author of your story.

Embrace Your Inner Action Hero: Think about your favorite action heroes from movies or books. What sets them apart? It's their unshakable drive, guts, and ability to face obstacles head-on. You too can reflect

These traits in your life. Embrace your inner action hero by understanding that you have the power to change your situations through your choices and actions.

Banishing the Waiting Game: Procrastination and waiting for the "right time" are typical roadblocks to taking action. The truth is, there's no right moment. The right time is now. Embracing a proactive approach means breaking free from the waiting game and jumping into action, even if it's a small step. Remember, success is made one step at a time.

The Joy of Ownership: Have you ever noticed how much more you respect something you've worked hard for? When you take an aggressive stance, you take ownership of your goals and dreams. This sense of control drives your desire and commitment. It's like growing a seed and watching it grow into a thriving tree that you tended with your own hands.

Simple Steps to Proactive Action: Set Clear Intentions: Define what you want to achieve and why it matters to you. Clarity of goal drives your energy.

Break it Down: Large chores can be stressful. Break them into smaller, doable steps. This makes the way forward less frightening.
Create a Plan: Outline your plan steps and make a schedule. A well-structured plan offers a path to follow.

Start Small: Begin with a small, doable job. Taking that initial step boosts your confidence and energy.
Stay Flexible: Life is uncertain. Be prepared to change your plan when needed, but never lose sight of your end goal.

Embracing Failure as Feedback: A proactive method isn't immune to mistakes, but it sees failures as stepping stones rather than roadblocks. Every mistake offers important lessons and feedback. Embrace mistakes as chances to learn, change, and grow stronger. Remember, even the most famous people faced mistakes on their trip.

A Supportive Environment: Surround yourself with people who encourage and inspire positive action. Share your goals with friends, family, or teachers who believe in your ability. Their help will keep you inspired and responsible.

In Conclusion: Shifting your viewpoint and taking a proactive approach is a powerful choice that will change your life. It's about taking charge of your fate, making chances, and never settle for failure. As you start on this trip, remember that every small action you take is a step toward the life you imagine. Get ready to watch your dreams change into reality as you accept the magic of being an Action Taker.

So, what's your first step going to be? Are you ready to shift your viewpoint and start on this exciting journey of strategic action-taking? The choice is yours, and the trip starts now.

The Psychology of Motivation: Igniting the Fire Within to Drive Action

Motivation is like the spark that starts a fire within us, pushing us to take action, achieve our goals, and make our dreams a reality. It's that inner drive that pushes us forward even when obstacles emerge. In this chapter, we'll dive into the interesting world of motivation and discover simple yet effective ways to tap its power and become action-takers in our everyday lives.

Understanding the Motivation Puzzle

Picture inspiration as a puzzle made up of different bits – each adding to our total drive. These pieces include our wants, goals, beliefs, and even our past events. But the most important piece of this puzzle is the "why" – the reason behind what we want to achieve. When we understand our "why," we fill our actions with purpose, making them more important and appealing.

Setting Clear Goals

To spark the fire of inspiration, we need clear and realistic goals. Goals serve as our roadmaps, leading us towards our preferred location. When making goals, remember the SMART criteria: Specific, Measurable, Achievable, Relevant, and Time-bound. For example, instead of saying, "I want to get fit," you could set the goal, "I will jog for 20 minutes every morning for the next month to improve my fitness."

Finding Your Passion

Passion is a powerful fuel for drive. Think about what things make you lose track of time, where you feel fully involved and passionate. These are often clues to your interests. When we match our goals

With our hobbies, the trip becomes more fun, and our drive skyrockets.

Visualizing Success

Close your eyes and imagine achieving your goal. How does it feel? Visualization is a powerful tool that tricks our brain into thinking we've already won. This positive feedback improves our confidence and drive, making us more likely to take action to turn our ideas into reality.

Overcoming Obstacles

Obstacles are unavoidable, but they don't have to stop us. Shift your viewpoint and view barriers as chances for growth. Break down your goals into smaller, doable steps. Celebrate each small win along the way, strengthening your drive to keep going.

Surrounding Yourself with Positivity

Surroundings play a major part in our drive. Connect with people who support and boost you. Engage in tasks that excite and energize you. Minimize exposure to negative and self-doubt, as they can dull your drive.

The Power of Rewards
Rewards act as quick satisfaction, strengthening the brain's positive link with a job. Treat yourself when you reach goals – it could be a small treat, a movie night, or a day off. Rewards build a sense of achievement and keep the inspiration spark going.

Cultivating Self-Discipline
Motivation isn't consistent, but self-discipline is. Create habits and stick to them. Even on days when inspiration seems elusive, your focused habits will move you forward. Consistency is key to long-term success.

Embracing Failures as Learning Opportunities
Failure is not the end; it's a stepping stone. Embrace mistakes as chances to learn and improve. The lessons you gain from failures will increase your drive and desire to try again.

Gratitude and Positive Affirmations
Practicing thanks and using positive mantras can significantly impact your drive. Start or end your day by recognizing what you're grateful for and praising your skills. Positive self-talk builds a strong attitude that's eager to take action.

Remember, drive is like a muscle – it can be taught and developed. By understanding the science behind motivation and following these simple techniques, you can constantly spark the fire within, moving you to take action, beat challenges, and achieve your goals. So, go ahead, fan the fire of inspiration, and start on your journey towards a more satisfying and accomplished life!

Chapter 2
Breaking the Chains of Procrastination

Welcome to Chapter 2 of our exciting trip in 'Get Things Done: The Action Taker's Guide to Overcoming Excuses'. In this chapter, we're going to face one of the most known obstacles to work and success: procrastination. We'll dig deep into understanding why we delay and, more importantly, arm you with practical and friendly strategies to break free from its grip and become a bold Action Taker.

Understanding Procrastination: The Sneaky Culprit

Picture this: you have a task on your to-do list, and you keep telling yourself, "I'll do it later." Sound familiar? That's laziness, the art of avoiding things that need to be done. Procrastination often comes in when we're faced with jobs that feel overwhelming, boring, or outside our comfort zones. It's like a sneaky enemy that can hinder your progress and rob you of precious time.

The Procrastination Paradox: Instant Gratification vs. Long-Term Success

Why do we procrastinate? Well, our brains are made to seek happiness and avoid pain. That's why binge-watching your favorite show or looking through social media feels so enticing in the moment. It's quick satisfaction. However, giving in to these distractions leads to delayed achievements and sorrow later on.

Procrastination-Busting Techniques: Your Action Plan

Mindful Awareness: The first step in beating delay is recognizing when it's happening. Tune in to your thoughts and feelings when you're tempted to put things off. Acknowledging your tendency to delay is the initial step towards change.

Break It Down: Large jobs can feel overwhelming, causing delay. Break them into smaller, doable parts. Instead of thinking, "I have to write a whole report," tell yourself, "I'll work on the introduction for 15 minutes." This makes the job less overwhelming.

Use the Two-Minute Rule: If a job takes less than two minutes to finish, do it quickly. Whether it's

Answering to an email or cleaning your desk, this simple rule stops small chores from piling up.

Set a Timer: The Pomodoro Technique is a lifesaver. Set a timer for 25 minutes, work on a job with full attention, then treat yourself with a 5-minute break. Repeat. It's like a mini-challenge that makes work feel less stressful.

picture Success: Close your eyes and picture how great it will feel to finish the job. Imagine the feeling of achievement and relaxation. This mental picture can improve desire and drive you to start.

Find Your Peak Productivity Time: Are you a morning person or do you shine in the evening? Identify your most effective time and plan difficult jobs during those hours.

Create a Procrastination-Free Zone: Designate a particular place for work without distractions. Turn off messages, put your phone on quiet, and make a setting that supports attention.

Your Procrastination-Free Future

Congratulations! You've just taken a big leap toward breaking free from procrastination's chains. Remember, growth, no matter how small, is a step in the right way. By adopting these easy and helpful strategies, you're opening the way to becoming an Action Taker who gets things done. So, go ahead, start small, and watch your successes grow as you bid goodbye to procrastinating and accept a more purposeful, satisfying life.

Understanding the Science Behind Procrastination and Its Impact

Procrastination – we've all been there, right? You know that feeling when you have a job looming over you, but you somehow find yourself looking through social media or cleaning out your room instead. It's like a sneaky guest that creeps in and steals away your precious time and output. But fear not, because in this chapter, we're going to dig into the science behind delay, uncover its secrets, and give you with simple yet effective strategies to beat its grasp.

The Procrastination Puzzle: Why Do We Do It?

Procrastination isn't just about being lazy or uninspired. It's based in our brain's complex processes. You see, our brains have evolved to seek happiness and avoid pain. When faced with a job that seems difficult or unpleasant, our brain's reward center doesn't light up like it does when we engage in fun activities. This is where delay sneaks in – it's our brain's way of finding instant satisfaction and avoiding pain.

Instant Gratification vs. Long-Term Rewards

Imagine you have a task due in a week. You know you should start early, but your brain says, "Hey, watching funny cat videos is way more fun right now." That's because your brain values the quick pleasure of cat videos over the delayed benefit of finishing your task. This quick satisfaction monkey (as humorously named by Tim Urban in his TED Talk) can derail your best plans and send you sliding into procrastination.

The Impact of Procrastination: More Than Just Time Lost

Procrastination isn't just about wasting time. It can have a domino effect on different parts of your life:

Stress and Anxiety: As deadlines approach, the stress of unfinished jobs can lead to anxiety, hurting your general well-being.

Reduced Quality: Rushing to finish a job at the last minute often leads to poor results, reducing the quality of your work.

Missed chances: Procrastination can cause you to miss out on chances, whether it's a raise at work or interesting events in your personal life.

Strained Relationships: Unfinished chores can spill over into your contacts with others, causing anger and pressure in relationships.

Simple Strategies to Beat Procrastination

Now that you understand the science behind delay and its effect, let's arm you with simple, friendly techniques to beat it:

Break it Down: Divide jobs into smaller, doable steps. Your brain loves a sense of achievement, even from the smallest wins.

Set a Timer: Use the Pomodoro Technique – work for 25 minutes, then take a 5-minute break. Rinse and repeat. It keeps your brain focused and driven.

Reward Yourself: Pair a job you're avoiding with something you love. Finish writing that report, then treat yourself to your favorite snack.

Visualize Success: Imagine the pleasure of finishing the task and the rewards it will bring.

Create a Procrastination-Free Zone: Designate a clutter-free, distraction-free area to improve focus.

Remember, you're not alone in this battle. Procrastination is a global challenge, but armed with the knowledge of its inner workings and armed with these user-friendly techniques, you're well on your way to taking control of your time and productivity. So, go ahead – show that quick satisfaction monkey who's boss and watch your successes soar!

Proven Techniques to Beat Procrastination and Take Swift Action

We've all been there – a looming job, a date inching closer, and yet, the strong urge to put it off for later. Procrastination, that sneaky foe, can hinder our progress and rob us of precious time. But fear not! In this chapter, we'll dig into some tried-and-true

Techniques that will help you beat procrastination and become a master of action-taking. Let's dive in!

Chunk It Down: The Micro-Task Approach

Imagine climbing a mountain: If you look at the top, it feels frightening. But if you focus on each step, the trip becomes doable. Apply this idea to your tasks. Break them into bite-sized chunks. Instead of "Write a report," try "Outline introduction," "Gather data," and "Draft conclusion." Smaller jobs are less scary and easier to start.

Set a Timer: The Pomodoro Technique

Work, but not too much: Set a timer for 25 minutes and engage yourself in a job. When the timer rings, take a 5-minute break. Repeat the cycle. This method keeps you focused and stops burnout. It's like a mini-challenge – can you stay on track for just 25 minutes?

Visualize Completion: The End-Result Imagery

See the finish line: Close your eyes and imagine the joy of finishing the job. How accomplished you'll feel! Visualization feeds drive and lowers the urge to wait. Your mind starts linking the task with happiness.

Deadline Mindset: The Self-Imposed Due Date
Trick your brain: Set an earlier limit than the real one. This taps into our natural desire to meet goals. You'll find yourself working harder to finish on time, reducing the desire to wait.

Reward System: The Sweet Incentive
Promise a treat: Give yourself a prize after finishing a job. It could be a favorite snack, a short YouTube break, or a walk outside. Your brain learns that action leads to pleasure, making you more likely to start right away.

Mind Dump: The Brain Clearing Technique
Unload your mind: Often, delay occurs because chores clutter our thoughts. Write down every job, no matter how small. This clears mind room and helps you focus on what needs doing.

Accountability Buddy: The Partner in Crime
Join forces: Share your tasks with a friend who's working on their to-do list. Regular check-ins create a sense of duty. You won't want to report unfinished jobs, so you'll be more likely to get things done.

Change of Scenery: The Fresh Start
Move around: A different setting can break the boredom and spark inspiration. If you're stuck, move – to a park, a café, or just another room. The change can help you beat the urge to wait.

Negative Reinforcement: The Consequence Rule
Create consequences: Assign a penalty if you don't start a job within a set limit. Maybe you skip your favorite show or give to a cause you don't support. The fear of bad results pushes you to act.

Self-Compassion: The Kind Approach
Be gentle with yourself: Understand that everyone faces delay. Instead of self-criticism, practice self-compassion. Treat yourself like a friend – with understanding and support.

Remember, taking action is a habit, and like all habits, it takes practice. Experiment with these methods, mix and match, and find what works best for you. Overcoming procrastination is like growing a muscle – the more you practice it, the stronger it becomes. So, go ahead, take that first step, and watch the urge to wait melt away as you become a true action-taking winner!

Cultivating Discipline and Building a Consistent Work Ethic

Congratulations on your choice to dive into the world of focus and steady work ethic! This chapter is your guide to manage the often tricky seas of keeping on track, getting things done, and meeting your goals. Let's start on this trip together, shall we?

Embrace the Power of Routine

Think of habits as your trusty sidekicks on the path to success. These are the nice habits that keep you grounded and focused. Start small – pick one exercise, maybe a morning stretch or a short meditation, and fit it into your daily routine. Over time, add more elements to your routine, like giving specific blocks of time for work, breaks, exercise, and rest.

Set Clear Goals

Picture this: you're on a car trip with a goal in mind. Without a map or GPS, you're likely to get lost. Similarly, without clear goals, your journey towards building discipline can be pointless. Define your goals – they could be finishing a job, learning a new skill, or hitting a health milestone. Break these bigger goals into smaller, doable jobs. When you

Have a clear plan, you're more likely to stay disciplined and focused.

Chunk It Down

Ever heard the saying, "How do you eat an elephant? One bite at a time." Applying this mindset to your tasks makes them far less overwhelming. Divide your jobs into smaller, bite-sized parts. Tackling these mini-tasks step by step feels doable and keeps your drive alive.

Prioritize with Purpose

Imagine juggling multiple balls – some rubber, some glass. You'd favor catching the weak ones, right? Similarly, not all jobs are made equal. Use the Eisenhower Matrix: identify jobs as urgent/important, important/not urgent, urgent/not important, or neither. Focus on the important, whether they're goals, growth chances, or self-improvement tasks.

Create a Distraction-Free Zone

Distractions are like shiny things that lead you away from your goals. Designate a distraction-free zone – a real place and a specific time – for your job. Turn off messages, put your phone on quiet, and let your

Friends know you're in "productive mode." This boosts your chances of staying focused and keeping a steady work attitude.

Embrace the Pomodoro Technique
Meet your new work pal – the Pomodoro Technique! Set a timer for 25 minutes, work intensely, then take a 5-minute break. After four rounds, treat yourself with a longer break. This method combats stress, keeps you involved, and helps develop a steady work flow.

Celebrate Small Wins
Remember, it's not just about the goal – the trip counts too. Celebrate each small success. Completing a task? Treat yourself to a snack. Finishing a project? Maybe a movie night is in order. These mini-celebrations keep your feelings high and drive rising.

Learn to Say No Picture your time and energy as valuable gems. You wouldn't give them away to just anyone, would you? Learn to say no to activities, jobs, or plans that don't match with your goals. By protecting your resources, you can pour them into what truly counts.

Reflect and Adjust

Life isn't static, and neither are you. Regularly think on your progress. What's going well? What needs tweaking? Be open and change your tactics properly. Adapting to change is a sign of power, not weakness.

Embody Self-Compassion

Discipline doesn't mean being hard on yourself. It's about encouraging growth. Treat yourself kindly, like you would a friend. If you fall, recognize it, learn from it, and move forward. A caring method ensures you keep going even when the road gets bumpy.

Remember, building focus and a steady work attitude is a journey. Each step you take, no matter how small, brings you closer to your goal. So, put up your spiritual climbing boots, pack your drive, and let's take the next step forward together! You've got this!

Chapter 3
From Excuses to Execution: Your Action Plan

Welcome to Chapter 3, where we're going deep into the heart of change – changing those goals and ideas into tangible, real-world activities. It's time to bid goodbye to reasons and accept the exciting path of execution.

Crafting Your Action Plan
Let's start by making a plan that will guide you from where you are right now to where you want to be. Your action plan is like a GPS for your goals. Here's how to make it:

Clear Goals: Begin by outlining your goals. What do you want to achieve? Be specific, whether it's getting your dream job, starting a business, or writing a book. Break down bigger goals into smaller, doable steps.

Prioritize: Not all jobs are made equal. Identify which jobs are most important for your goal. Prioritization avoids overload and ensures you're working on what matters most.

Actionable Steps: Now, let's get real. Break each goal into doable steps. Instead of "Write a book," it's "Write 500 words every day." Make these steps as clear as a recipe – so easy that anyone could follow them.

The Two-Minute Rule: If a job takes less than two minutes, do it quickly. This simple trick stops small jobs from piling up.

Set dates: Assign dates to each step. Deadlines create a sense of urgency and prevent delay. Remember, dates aren't enemies; they're your responsibility friends.

Visualize Success: Close your eyes and imagine reaching your goal. Feel the feelings, hear the cheers. Visualization primes your mind for success.

Chunking: Divide your action steps into small chunks of time. Maybe it's 25 minutes of focused work (hello, Pomodoro Technique!) followed by a 5-minute break. Small, steady efforts bring big effects.

Overcoming Excuses

Excuses are like rocks stopping your way. But here's how to break them down:

Awareness: Catch yourself making reasons. Are you saying, "I'll start tomorrow" or "I don't have time"? Recognize these reasons for what they are – barriers to growth.

Flip the Script: Transform excuses into reasons. Instead of "I don't have time," say, "I'll make time because this matters." Positive language encourages action.

Accountability: Share your action plan with a friend or instructor. Accountability partners keep you on track and celebrate your wins.

Progress Tracking

Celebrate each step forward, no matter how small. Progress drives desire. Here's how to track:

Checklists: Create a plan for each goal. Crossing things off is oddly rewarding and encourages you to keep going.

Journaling: Write about your progress. Reflect on obstacles and how you overcame them. Journaling is a personal pep talk.

Visual Progress: Use images like charts or graphs to see your progress. Watching those bars fill up is incredibly inspiring.

Course Correction
Life isn't a straight road. Expect delays and potholes. When things don't go as planned:

Adaptability: Embrace change. If a method isn't working, change it. Flexibility is your secret tool.

Learning Opportunity: Mistakes aren't mistakes; they're lessons. Analyze what went wrong and use that information to improve.

Resilience: Don't let failures define you. Bounce back stronger. Remember, every great person has a trail of mistakes behind them.

Remember, your action plan is your guide. It makes dreams into reality. So, arm yourself with drive, kill those excuses, and let's make things happen!

Crafting Your Action Plan: Turning Ideas into Action with Ease

Have you ever been filled with great ideas, only to find yourself stuck in the mud of inaction? Don't worry, you're not alone. Many of us have experienced the pain of having great ideas but failing to bring them to life. That's where creating a clear action plan comes in – your secret tool to bridge the gap between ideas and performance. In this chapter, we're going to dive into the nitty-gritty of making an action plan that is not only useful but also simple and friendly to your team. Let's get started!

Clarify Your Vision: Begin by clearly describing your idea or goal. What exactly do you want to achieve? Paint a clear idea of the end result in your thoughts. This focus will serve as your guide throughout the production process.

Break It Down: Big goals can be confusing. Break your idea down into smaller, doable jobs. Think of these jobs as moving stones towards your final goal. Each finished job gets you one step closer to success.

Set SMART Goals: Make your jobs Specific, Measurable, Achievable, Relevant, and Time-bound (SMART). This plan ensures your goals are clear, reasonable, and have a timeline. For instance, instead of saying "Write a book," a SMART goal could be "Write 500 words of the first chapter by Friday."

Prioritize jobs: Not all jobs are made equal. Determine which jobs have the biggest effect and handle those first. Prioritization stops you from getting lost in minor jobs and keeps you focused on what truly matters.

Create a schedule: Map out a schedule for each job and the general project. Be realistic about how much time each job will take. A well-structured schedule helps you stay on track and ensures you're making steady progress.

Allocate tools: Identify the tools you need for each job. This could be time, money, tools, or experience. Ensure that you have everything in place before you begin, so you can avoid pointless hiccups along the way.

Delegate Wisely: If you're working with a team, delegate tasks based on skills and experience. Delegation not only lightens your load but also strengthens your team members and encourages teamwork.

Take Small Steps: Sometimes, the hardest part is simply starting. Commit to taking a small, practical step each day. Whether it's writing a line, making a phone call, or doing research, these small steps build energy and prevent delay.

Monitor and Adjust: Regularly review your work. Are you sticking to your timeline? Are you facing any unexpected challenges? Adjust your action plan as needed. Flexibility is key to adapting to new situations.

enjoy Milestones: Don't forget to enjoy your successes along the way. Each finished task is a win worth recognizing. Treat yourself and your team to a small prize or praise when you hit goals.

Remember, making a clear action plan is like building a path to success. It's not about perfection; it's about growth. By breaking down your goals,

Setting clear targets, and taking consistent steps, you'll turn your ideas from mere thoughts into real achievements. So, grab a pen and paper (or your best digital tool) and start making your action plan today. Your journey from ideas to action starts now!

Goal Setting Techniques that Spark Immediate Action

Setting goals is like planning a course for your trip to success. However, the real magic happens when you turn those goals into acts that drive you forward. In this chapter, we'll study a set of goal-setting techniques that will not only excite you but also force you to take instant steps towards your dreams. Get ready to turn your goals into real results!

Start with Clear and Specific Goals
Vague goals are like puzzles missing key pieces. To spark action, your goals need to be crystal clear. Instead of saying, "I want to be healthier," try "I will walk for 30 minutes every morning to improve my fitness." Specificity draws a clear picture of what you want to achieve, making it easier to take the first step.

Break Big Goals into Small Steps
Big goals can be stressful, but breaking them down into smaller, doable steps turns them into bite-sized wins. Want to write a book? Begin by setting aside just 30 minutes each day to write a few lines. These mini-goals make your journey less overwhelming and more doable.

Create a Visual Roadmap
A picture is worth a thousand words, and a visual image of your goals can be a strong motivation. Create a vision board or a digital collage that shows your desired results. Seeing your dreams in live color can spark joy and prompt you to take action to turn those ideas into reality.

Set Deadlines and Milestones
Without limits, goals often drift into the realm of "someday." Set clear goals for each step along your trip. Breaking your progress into benchmarks allows you to track your development and experience a feeling of success at regular times.

Use SMART Goals Technique
SMART stands for Specific, Measurable, Achievable, Relevant, and Time-bound. Applying

This method helps you create goals that are useful and appealing. For instance, "I will increase my monthly sales by 15% within the next six months by reaching out to five new clients every week."

Visualize Success

Close your eyes and imagine the moment you achieve your goal. Feel the feelings, hear the cheers, and experience the joy. This mental training not only boosts your drive but also pushes you to take the necessary actions to turn your vision into a concrete reality.

Use the Two-Minute Rule

If a job takes less than two minutes to finish, do it quickly. This simple rule stops small jobs from piling up and becoming overwhelming. By regularly handling quick jobs, you build energy and make a habit of taking action.

Build Accountability

Share your goals with a friend or family member who can provide support and hold you accountable. Knowing that someone is cheering you on can light a fire under you, pushing you to take those initial steps.

Reward Yourself
Celebrate your successes, no matter how small. Treat yourself to something enjoyable when you hit a milestone. These prizes build good links with your actions, making you more eager to take the next step.

Start Now, Adjust Along the Way
Perfection is the enemy of progress. Don't wait for the right time; start with what you have. You can improve your method as you go. The key is to begin and make changes as needed, rather than getting stuck in the loop of overthinking.

Remember, the trip of a thousand miles starts with a single step. By applying these friendly and straightforward goal-setting methods, you'll find yourself not only setting goals but also taking inspired action to bring your dreams to life. So, let's take that first step together and start on a path of important achievement!

How to Track Progress and Stay Accountable to Yourself

Congratulations on starting on your journey to become an Action Taker! One of the key pillars to meeting your goals and reaching your dreams is tracking your progress and keeping yourself responsible. In this chapter, we'll dive deep into simple and effective methods to help you stay on track, measure your improvements, and celebrate your wins along the way. Let's get started!

The Magic of Tracking Progress
Imagine building a puzzle. Each piece you join brings you closer to finishing the picture. Similarly, tracking growth is like putting together your personal success puzzle. It helps you to see how far you've come, what's left to be done, and the road you need to follow. Here's how you can do it:

Set Clear Milestones
Break down your bigger goals into smaller, doable steps. These milestones act as guideposts, letting you see your progress more clearly. For instance, if your goal is to write a book, your milestones could be finishing each chapter.

Keep a Journal or Progress Tracker
Maintain a notebook, calendar, or even a simple note-taking app to record your daily or weekly progress. This can be as simple as jotting down what you achieved, obstacles you faced, and any insights gained.

Visualize Your Progress
Create a graphic picture of your work. This could be a checklist, a graph, or a vision board that displays your accomplishments. Visual cues can be highly inspiring and rewarding.

Regular Review
Set aside focused time to review your work. Weekly or monthly check-ins help you to examine what's working, what's not, and make necessary changes.

The Art of Self-Accountability
Staying responsible to yourself requires commitment and a soft yet strong approach. Let's explore how you can keep this commitment:

Set Clear Goals
Clarity is your best friend. Define your goals in clear, measurable terms. Instead of saying, "I want

To get fit," say, "I want to jog for 30 minutes every morning."

Create a Routine
Consistency is key. Establish a practice that fits with your goals. A set plan makes it easier to organize chores and measure progress.

Find an Accountability Buddy
Share your goals with a friend or family member who can offer support and hold you responsible. Having someone to share your trip with makes it more pleasant.

Reward Yourself
Treat yourself for hitting goals. Rewards provide positive feedback and keep you driven. Just remember to choose prizes that match with your goals.

Reflect and Adjust
Regularly measure your progress. Celebrate successes, learn from failures, and change your method as needed. This isn't about greatness; it's about ongoing growth.

Celebrate Your Wins
Every step forward is a win worth celebrating. Acknowledge your successes, no matter how small they may seem. Celebrating boosts your mood and strengthens your resolve.

Stay Patient and Kind to Yourself
Remember, improvement takes By tracking your progress and adopting self-accountability, you're setting yourself up for success. The road to your goals might have twists and turns, but with drive, steady effort, and the right tools, you'll become a master at tracking progress and achieving what you set out to accomplish. Keep up the great work, and enjoy the trip to becoming the Action Taker you're meant to be!

Chapter 4
Embracing Challenges and Overcoming Setbacks

Life is an uncertain journey filled with changes, turns, and surprising obstacles. In this chapter, we're going to dig deep into the art of accepting these difficulties and triumphing over failures. Remember, every failure is a chance for a comeback, and by developing the right attitude and choosing effective strategies, you can turn hurdles into stepping stones on your path to success.

The Mindset of Resilience

Embracing difficulties starts with having a strong attitude. Instead of viewing losses as fails, see them as important lessons. Understand that mistakes are not signs of your worth or promise, but simply times of adjustment. Embrace the attitude that every task you face is a chance to learn, grow, and become better.

Reframing Setbacks

When faced with failures, learn the art of rethinking. Look at the problem from different sides and ask yourself: What can I learn from this? How can I use this knowledge to my advantage? By viewing failures as chances for growth, you change your attention from dwelling on the negative to taking the positive.

Creating a Resilience Plan

Prepare yourself for difficulties by making a recovery plan. Think of it as your tools for beating setbacks. Identify possible hurdles in your journey and describe practical steps you can take to move through them. Having a plan in place gives you with the courage and understanding to face obstacles head-on.

Adapting and Flexibility

In a constantly changing world, flexibility is key. Embrace the idea that things may not always go as planned, and that's okay. Stay fluid in your approach and be open to changing your tactics. Remember, it's not about avoiding difficulties, but about how you move through them.

Learning from Failure

Failure is a normal part of any journey towards success. Instead of fearing loss, accept it as a stepping stone. When failures appear, take the time to examine what went wrong and extract useful insights. Apply these lessons to hone your method and improve your chances of success in the future.

Seeking Support

You're not in this journey alone. Don't fear to seek help from friends, family, teachers, or even support groups. Sharing your problems with others can provide fresh views and answers you might not have considered. Additionally, knowing that you have a support system can improve your mood and help you stay focused.

Cultivating Patience

Overcoming setbacks often takes patience. Rome wasn't built in a day, and neither is your way to success. Understand that success takes time and failures are just temporary roadblocks. Cultivate

Patience as you work hard towards your goals, enjoying every small win along the way.

Visualization and Positive Affirmations

Visualize yourself conquering obstacles and achieving your goals. Use positive mantras to improve your confidence and keep an upbeat attitude, even in the face of setbacks. Your mind is a powerful tool, and by mastering its potential, you can create the strength and grit needed to conquer obstacles.

Remember, every failure you beat brings you one step closer to your dreams. Embrace obstacles as chances for growth, and let your drive shine as you move through life's twists and turns. By learning the art of conquering setbacks, you're not just building a successful life – you're becoming a stronger, smarter, and more adaptable individual who can conquer anything that comes your way.

Navigating Roadblocks and Setbacks with Resilience and Determination

Life is a trip filled with changes and turns, and it's not always smooth sailing. Along the way, you'll face roadblocks and failures that can feel depressing and overwhelming. But fear not, because in this chapter, we're going to give you with the tools, attitude, and strategies you need to handle these challenges with grit and unwavering drive.

Embrace the Mindset of Resilience:

Resilience is like your inner fighter – it's the ability to bounce back and keep going, even when things get tough. The first step is to accept that failures are a normal part of any journey. They're not signs of failure but chances to learn and grow. So, when you meet a roadblock, take a deep breath, tell yourself that mistakes happen to everyone, and focus on what you can learn from the situation.

Break it Down:

When faced with a big, frightening roadblock, it's easy to feel stressed. The trick is to break it down

Into smaller, doable steps. Think of it as climbing a peak – you don't look at the top and get frustrated; you focus on the next step. Write down the specific challenges you're having, and then plan realistic steps you can take to solve each one. As you finish these smaller steps, you'll gain a sense of success and energy.

Tap into Your Support Network:

You're not in this alone. Reach out to your friends, family, teachers, or peers for help. Talking about your difficulties can provide fresh views and ideas that you might not have considered. Plus, sharing your problems makes you understand that others have faced similar roadblocks and emerged better. Remember, asking for help isn't a sign of weakness; it's a sign of strength and a proof to your desire to beat hurdles.

Cultivate Flexibility:

Resilience doesn't mean firmly sticking to one road, regardless of the circumstances. It's about being flexible and open to changing your plans. If a roadblock makes your original method impossible,

Imagine alternative paths. Being open in your thinking helps you to find creative answers and keep going forward.

Celebrate Small Wins:

In the face of setbacks, it's easy to focus on what's going wrong. Instead, change your viewpoint and enjoy your small wins. Did you beat a small obstacle? Did you make progress on a difficult task? Celebrate these wins, no matter how small they may seem. This confidence will fuel your drive and inspire you to keep going forward.

Learn and Grow:

Every failure holds a lesson. After you've overcome a roadblock, take time to think on what you've learned. What worked? What didn't? How can you apply these lessons in the future? This growth attitude turns obstacles into useful experiences that add to your personal and professional development.

Practice Self-Care:

Resilience isn't just about pushing through obstacles; it's also about taking care of yourself. When faced with roadblocks, worry can mount, hurting your physical and mental well-being. Engage in activities that refresh you – whether it's exercise, relaxing, spending time with loved ones, or engaging in a skill. Remember, taking care of yourself is an important part of staying strong.

Visualize Success:

Use the power of your mind to picture yourself beating the roadblocks and reaching your goals. Create a mental picture of yourself pushing through obstacles with drive and emerging victorious. This positive image boosts your confidence and drive, making it easier to stay strong when faced with challenges.

Stay Patient and Persistent:

Resilience takes patience and determination. Some roadblocks may take longer to handle than others, but that doesn't mean you should give up. Stay committed to your goals, keep taking small steps,

And tell yourself that failures are temporary. Your determination will pay off in the end.

Keep Your Eye on the Prize:

Amidst roadblocks, it's easy to lose sight of your end goal. Create a clear reminder of your goal – a vision board, a note on your desk, or a digital background. Whenever you feel discouraged, look at this lesson and reunite with your purpose. It will reignite your drive and give you the strength to endure.

Remember, failures are not roadblocks – they're merely detours on your trip to success. By adopting resilience and determination, you have the power to handle these obstacles and emerge stronger, smarter, and more determined than ever before. So, keep your chin up, take a deep breath, and let your unshakable spirit guide you through any storm. You've got this!

Turning Failures into Stepping Stones Toward Success

Hey there, fellow Action Taker! We all know that life is a wild ride, full of ups and downs. Sometimes, things don't go as expected, and we find ourselves facing what might seem like a loss. But guess what? Failure is not the end of the road; it's a pit stop on the way to success. Let's dig into how you can turn those mistakes into stepping stones that lead you straight to your dreams.

Embrace the Lesson

First things first, don't be too hard on yourself. Failing is not a measure of your worth or skills. It's a lesson – a useful one at that. Take a deep breath and ask yourself, "What can I learn from this experience?" Maybe you found a plan that didn't work, or you learned something new about yourself. Embracing the lesson is like getting a valuable bit of knowledge that you can take forward.

Analyze and Reflect

Once you've caught that rare rock, it's time to think. Sit down with a notebook or your favorite note-taking app and jot down what went wrong. Was it a lack of preparation? Did you forget some important details? Identifying the root reasons of the loss will enable you to avoid making the same mistakes in the future.

Adjust Your Course

Alright, you've got the lesson, and you've examined the case. Now, it's time to make changes. Think of it like changing your sails when the wind changes direction. Adapt your method based on what you've learned. This is your chance to tweak your plan and make it even better.

Set Smarter Goals

Failures are great teachers when it comes to setting goals. Maybe your earlier goal was too lofty, or perhaps it wasn't specific enough. Use your loss to set better goals – ones that are Specific, Measurable, Achievable, Relevant, and Time-bound (SMART). These goals give you a clear path and make success feel much more doable.

Stay Positive and Persistent

It's easy to feel discouraged after a loss, but remember, even the most successful people faced mistakes. The key is to keep a good mood and stay determined. Believe in your ability to beat obstacles. Use mantras, surround yourself with encouraging people, and remember yourself of your past successes. You've got this!

Seek Support and Learn

Don't be afraid to ask for help. Whether it's a guide, a friend, or an online group, finding help can provide fresh views and insights. Learning from others who've been through similar situations can be incredibly useful. They might share methods you haven't thought of or give you the support you need to keep going.

Celebrate Small Wins

As you make progress, enjoy every small win along the way. These wins are like the signs that lead you out of the woods of failure. Celebrating boosts your

Confidence and drive, making you more strong in the face of difficulties.

Keep Trying, Keep Growing

Turning mistakes into stepping stones toward success is a constant process. Remember, success is not a goal; it's an ongoing journey. Keep trying, keep growing, and keep making those stumbling blocks into building blocks for your dreams.

So there you have it, dear Action Taker. When life throws lemons at you, don't just make lemonade – build a lemonade business! Embrace mistakes, learn from them, and use them as stepping stones that raise you to greater heights. Your success story is being written with every task you conquer. Keep going forward, and remember, the trip itself is a beautiful part of the success you're meant for.

The Art of Adapting and Thriving in the Face of Adversity

Life is a trip filled with ups and downs, changes and turns. Adversity is an essential part of this trip, but it doesn't have to define us. Instead of allowing

Obstacles to hold us back, we can learn the art of adjusting and growing in the face of hardship. This is where true strength and growth are developed.

Embrace Change as a Friend
Adversity often comes in the form of sudden changes - a job loss, a breakup, a health issue. The first step in adjusting is to accept that change is a normal part of life. Embrace it as a chance for growth rather than a hurdle. Remember, every loss can be a setup for a comeback.

Action Tip: When faced with sudden change, take a deep breath, and tell yourself that you have the power to move through it.

Maintain a Positive Mindset
Your attitude is your best tool in facing hardship. Cultivate a good outlook by focusing on what you can control rather than what you can't. Look for the silver lining in every situation and remember yourself of past difficulties you've defeated. A optimistic attitude can boost your flexibility.

Action Tip: Start a thanks book. Write down three things you're thankful for every day, even in tough times.

Flexibility is Key

Adapting takes flexibility. Just like a tree moves with the wind, we too must be ready to bend and change our plans. Don't be afraid to turn and discover new roads. Often, the most beautiful finds come from surprising stops.

Action Tip: The next time a plan doesn't go as planned, brainstorm alternative ways and be open to trying a different method.

Break it Down

Adversity can feel overwhelming when viewed as a whole. Break down obstacles into smaller, doable steps. Focus on taking one step at a time. This not only makes the situation less scary but also gives you a sense of success with each milestone you hit.

Action Tip: Create a plan of tasks to handle a difficult scenario. Celebrate each small win along the way.

Seek Support

You don't have to face hardship alone. Seek help from friends, family, or experts. Sharing your problems and getting advice can provide you with fresh views and the mental boost you need.

Action Tip: Reach out to a trusted friend and let them know what you're going through. Sometimes, talking it out can lead to ideas you hadn't considered.

Learn and Adapt

Adversity is a great teacher. Take time to think on what you've learned from difficult scenarios. Use these lessons to change and make informed choices going forward. Your ability to learn and change will set you up for success.

Action Tip: After beating a tough situation, write about the lessons you've learned and how you'll apply them in the future.

Practice Self-Care

In times of hardship, self-care becomes even more important. Nurture your physical, social, and spiritual well-being. Engage in things that bring you

Joy and rest. When you take care of yourself, you're better prepared to face obstacles head-on.

Action Tip: Dedicate at least 15 minutes a day to an activity that helps you relax, whether it's reading, resting, or going for a walk.

Celebrate Progress
Amid hardship, celebrate even the smallest successes. Acknowledging your progress boosts your confidence and pushes you to keep going. Remember, every step forward is a win.

Action Tip: Treat yourself to something special when you hit a milestone. It could be as easy as having your favorite snack or taking a day off to relax.

Embrace Resilience
Resilience is the cornerstone of changing and thriving in hardship. It's not about avoiding difficulties but about having the strength to bounce back. Embrace setbacks as chances to build your endurance muscle.

Action Tip: Create a statement or phrase that tells you of your resilience, such as "I am strong and capable of overcoming anything."

Keep the Vision Alive
In the middle of hardship, it's easy to lose sight of your goals and dreams. Keep your idea alive and let it guide your actions. Your dreams can provide the inspiration and direction you need to endure.

Action Tip: Create a vision board with pictures and words that describe your goals. Place it somewhere you'll see it daily.

Adapting and growing in the face of hardship is a journey of self-discovery and strength. By accepting change, keeping a positive attitude, and taking small, intentional steps, you'll not only manage obstacles but emerge stronger and more adaptable than ever before. Remember, you have the power to not only escape hardship but to grow in its middle.

Chapter 5
Time Mastery: Making Every Moment Count

Welcome to Chapter 5 of our action-packed trip in "Get Things Done." In this chapter, we're digging into the interesting world of Time Mastery – a skill that will help you squeeze every drop of productivity and joy from your day, without feeling stressed. So, grab your best beverage, sit in, and let's uncover the secrets of making every moment count!

Section 1: Understanding the Time Puzzle

Hey there, time traveler! Before we start on this exciting adventure, let's take a moment to understand the nature of time. Time isn't just a running clock; it's your most valuable resource. Think of it as a puzzle waiting to be solved. We'll help you understand it piece by piece.

Time Awareness: Imagine you have a special clock that counts down the seconds of your life. Well, surprise – you do! It's called your daily plan. Start by tracking how you spend your time each day. This eye-opening practice will show where your minutes vanish and where you can take control.

Prioritization Magic: Now that you know where your time goes, let's make some prioritization magic. Jot down your jobs for the day, and give each an importance score. This simple act will guide you to focus on what truly counts.

Section 2: The Art of Smart Scheduling

Buckle up, time virtuoso! We're about to explore the art of smart organizing, where boring chores and important goals live in perfect harmony.

Time Blocking: Picture your day as a painting. Instead of a messy mix of jobs, make colored blocks of focused time. Dedicate chunks to specific tasks, whether it's work, exercise, or spending important time with a loved one. Remember, each block has a reason, and you're the master.

The Magic of Routines: Ever wished you had a magic wand to make habits stick? Well, we've got the next best thing: habit creation. Start small – commit to a morning routine that sets a good tone for your day. Whether it's a short meditation, a brisk walk, or a healthy breakfast, regular habits create a flow that keeps you dancing through your day.

Section 3: Taming the Distraction Dragon

Ah, distractions – the wicked dragons that steal your precious time. But fear not, brave soul! You're about to learn how to tame these beasts and reignite your focus.

Digital Detox Delight: Your gadgets are great tools, but they can also be time-gobbling monsters. Schedule small digital detoxes throughout your day. Power down, unplug, and enjoy the freedom from computers. Your mind will thank you!

Focus Fuels Productivity: Imagine you're baking a cake. You can't rush the process, or you'll end up with a soggy mess. The same goes for your chores. Embrace the Pomodoro Technique: set a timer for 25 minutes of focused attention, followed by a 5-minute break. Rinse and repeat. Watch your output rise like a paper airplane.

Section 4: Making Time for You

You've juggled jobs, tamed distractions, and time-blocked like a pro. Now, it's time to love yourself.

Me Time Mandate: Remember, you're not a machine. To keep your gears well-oiled, commit times in your plan solely to yourself. Read a book, take an outdoor walk, or simply breathe. Your well-being is your strength.

think and Recharge: As your day winds down, take a few moments to think. What did you achieve? What challenges did you overcome? Celebrate your wins, no matter how small. They're the stepping stones to your bigger success.

Congratulations, time wizard! You've finished Chapter 5, and you're well on your way to learning the art of making every moment count. Remember, each tick of the clock is a chance to create a beauty of efficiency and satisfaction. So go ahead, grab that amazing timer – your journey continues!

Strategies for Optimizing Your Time and Maximizing Productivity

Time is a valuable resource, and how we use it can greatly affect our success and satisfaction. In this chapter, we'll dive into useful and Easy-to-implement strategies that will help you improve your time and boost your output.

Prioritize with Purpose
Start your day by finding the most important jobs that need your attention. Use the Eisenhower Matrix: identify jobs as urgent/important, important/not urgent, urgent/not important, or neither. Focus on the jobs that fall into the "important" group, as these add greatly to your long-term goals.

Time Blocking
Divide your day into blocks of time, each committed to a specific job or type of work. This method helps you stay focused and avoid juggling, which can lead to waste. Set clear start and end times for each block, and don't forget to include short breaks to recharge.

Eliminate Time-Wasters
Identify tasks that take your time without adding value. Limit social media reading, limit delays, and share chores that can be handled by others. Be aware of activities that drain your time and energy.

Set SMART Goals
Utilize the SMART (Specific, Measurable, Achievable, Relevant, Time-bound) strategy to set clear goals. Specific goals provide direction, measured goals allow you to track progress, and time-bound goals create a sense of pressure.

Use the Two-Minute Rule
If a job can be finished in two minutes or less, handle it quickly. This stops small jobs from piling up and becoming overwhelming.

Batch Similar Tasks
Group similar jobs together and handle them in a single time. Respond to emails, make phone calls, or finish routine work in specific time blocks. This reduces topic switching and improves attention.

Limit Decision Fatigue
Reduce the number of choices you need to make each day. Plan your clothes, meals, and everyday routines in advance. This frees up brain energy for more important choices.

Use Technology Wisely

Leverage efficiency apps and tools to streamline your chores. Calendar apps, job planners, and note-taking apps can help you stay organized and on track. However, be careful not to fall into the trap of endless app management.

Practice the Pomodoro Technique

Work hard for 25 minutes, then take a 5-minute break. After four rounds, take a longer break. This method boosts attention and stops burnout.

Learn to Say No

Respectfully reject jobs or duties that don't fit with your goals or values. Saying no helps you protect your time and focus on what truly counts.

Delegate and Collaborate

Don't hesitate to assign chores to others, whether at work or home. Effective delegating frees up your time for chores that require your knowledge.

Reflect and Adjust

Regularly examine your efficiency tactics. Celebrate your achievements and find places for improvement.

Adjust your method based on what works best for you.

Remember, saving your time isn't about working harder, but working better. By applying these tactics, you'll not only accomplish more but also make space for activities that bring you joy and satisfaction. Start small, try with different techniques, and gradually build a routine that improves your output while allowing you to lead a healthy and worthwhile life.

Techniques to Prioritize Tasks and Eliminate Time-Wasting Activities

Welcome to a chapter that holds the key to unlocking your time management skills! In this journey, we'll dive into practical and simple techniques that will empower you to take control of your schedule, plan tasks effectively, and bid goodbye to those sneaky time-wasting habits.

Your Task's Value: Start by learning the true value of each task. Ask yourself: Is this job important to my goals? Will finishing it bring me closer to success? Focus on high-value jobs that match with your goals, and share, delay, or discard the rest.

The Urgent-Important Matrix: Picture a 2x2 grid. Label the quadrants as Urgent & Important, Not Urgent & Important, Urgent & Not Important, and Not Urgent & Not Important. Place jobs properly. Tackle Urgent & Important jobs first, followed by Important but Not Urgent ones. Limit time spent on Urgent & Not Important jobs and avoid Not Urgent & Not Important activities.

Eat the Frogs: Imagine your chores as frogs. Your goal is to "eat" the biggest, ugly frog (the most difficult job) first thing in the morning. By completing the tough job early, you set a positive tone for the day and improve your confidence.

Time Blocking: Divide your day into blocks, each committed to specific jobs or types of work. This stops confusion, improves focus, and ensures you assign time for important activities.

The Pomodoro Technique: Work for 25 minutes, then take a 5-minute break. After four rounds, take a longer break. This method uses your brain's focus

Span, keeping output while giving you regular times to recover.

Eliminate Distractions: Identify your most common distractions and create tactics to lessen them. Silence alerts, clear your workspace, and use website blocks to keep your attention alive.

Two-Minute Rule: If a job takes two minutes or less, do it quickly. This stops small jobs from piling up and taking more time later.

Batching: Group similar jobs together and handle them in one go. For instance, answer texts during a set time slot rather than spread throughout the day. This reduces context-switching and improves productivity.

Limit Decision Fatigue: Reduce the number of choices you make each day by creating routines. Simplify choices like what to wear or eat, so you can put your mental energy into more critical decisions.

Regular Reviews: Periodically review your jobs and goals. Are you on track? Are there chores that can be removed or delegated? Adjust your goals as

Needed to ensure you're always connected with your aims.

Remember, learning time management is a journey. Implement one method at a time and notice what works best for you. Be kind to yourself, and enjoy your growth along the way. By following these simple yet powerful strategies, you'll find yourself with more time, improved output, and a fresh sense of satisfaction. So, are you ready to recover your time and conquer your tasks? Let's do this!

Creating a Balanced Routine for Maximum Efficiency and Well-Being

Hey there, fellow Action Taker! In this chapter, we're going into the exciting world of crafting a healthy routine that not only boosts your work but also supports your general well-being. We get it – life can be a balancing act, but with the right practice, you can achieve your goals while keeping your health. Let's break it down step by step in easy and nice terms:

Step 1: Start with Your Priorities

Sit down with a cup of your favorite brew – coffee, tea, or even hot chocolate – and give some thought to what truly matters to you. What are your big goals? Your passions? Your must-dos and want-to-dos? Jot them down. This list is like your personal guide leading you to build a habit that fits with your dreams.

Step 2: Plot Your Day

Think of your day as a surface waiting for your touches of purpose. Break it into chunks – morning, afternoon, evening. Allocate time blocks for your goals from Step 1. Whether it's work, exercise, family time, or self-care, make room for them.

Step 3: Embrace Flexibility

Life isn't a robotically planned business. Be open to changes. Sometimes, your dog decides to be your alarm clock, or your imagination strikes at unexpected times. Flexibility keeps your routine from feeling like a straitjacket.

Step 4: The Power of Morning Rituals

Mornings set the tone for your day. Consider a routine that sparks happiness – stretching, writing, meditation, or even dancing to your favorite tune.

These small acts boost your happiness and prepare you to face the day.

Step 5: Work Smarter, Not Harder
Productivity isn't about clocking endless hours. It's about focused, successful work. Chunk your jobs into reasonable time blocks, and take short breaks in between. Ever heard of the Pomodoro Technique? It's like a game of work and prize.

Step 6: Nourish and Move Your Body
Remember, you're not a robot. Your body needs food and exercise. Whip up a healthy breakfast – oatmeal with berries, anyone? And make time for a walk, exercise, or whatever gets your blood moving.

Step 7: Quality Time with Loved Ones
Family and friends are the spice of life. Allocate times for them – a filling dinner, a call, or even a silly text conversation. These interactions recharge you mentally.

Step 8: Me Time is Essential
Yes, you earn a slice of your day too. This is your time to read, binge-watch, paint, or whatever floats your boat. Remember, a happy you is a busy you.

Step 9: Wind Down Gracefully
As the day winds down, wind down too. Disconnect from screens an hour before bed – this helps you sleep better. Read a book, practice thanks, or simply relax.

Step 10: Sleep, Glorious Sleep
Your pattern ends in the cocoon of sleep. Prioritize it. Create a relaxing sleep routine – dim lights, a cozy blanket, maybe some light music. Your body and mind will thank you.

Step 11: Review and Adjust
Regularly peek at your practice. Is it working for you? Are you thriving? Tweak where needed. Your habit is like a plant – it needs care and trimming to grow.

Remember, friend, balance is the key. Your routine is like a symphony – each note (action) plays a part in making a beautiful song (your life). So, go on, make a habit that brings out the best in you. You've got this!

Chapter 6
Overpowering Distractions and Staying Focused

Welcome to Chapter 6 of your action-packed journey in "Get Things Done: The Action Taker's Guide to Overcoming Excuses"! Here, we're diving into the exciting world of overcoming distractions and mastering the art of unwavering focus.

Section 1: Understanding the Distraction Dilemma

Picture this: You sit down with all the right intentions, ready to tackle that important task. But suddenly, your phone buzzes, a notification pops up, and before you know it, you're lost in a sea of distractions. Sound familiar? We've all been there. Distractions are sneaky little critters that can derail your progress and rob you of precious time.

Section 2: Declutter Your Space, Boost Your Mind

Creating a distraction-free environment is your secret weapon to staying focused. Start by organizing your workspace. A tidy desk equals a tidy mind. Keep only the essentials in sight – your

Tools, a glass of water, and maybe a motivational quote to keep you going.

Section 3: The Magic of the Pomodoro Technique

Now, let's talk about the Pomodoro Technique, a game-changer for your productivity. It's as simple as setting a timer for 25 minutes, focusing solely on your task, and then rewarding yourself with a 5-minute break. Rinse and repeat. This technique harnesses the power of focused bursts and helps you stay on track without feeling overwhelmed.

Section 4: Mindfulness Meditation for Laser Focus

Ever heard of mindfulness meditation? It's like a mental gym session. Spend just a few minutes each day sitting comfortably, focusing on your breath, and letting go of those nagging thoughts. This practice trains your brain to ignore distractions and brings your attention back to the task at hand. It's like building a mental muscle of focus!

Section 5: Unleash Your Inner Sherlock: Identify Distraction Sources

Become a detective of your distractions. Is it social media, chatty colleagues, or the allure of funny cat videos? Once you identify your distractions, you can create strategies to combat them. Turn off notifications, set specific times for checking emails, or create a "do not disturb" sign during your focused work sessions.

Section 6: Setting Focused Intentions

Before you dive into your task, set a clear intention. What do you want to accomplish during this focused time? Write it down, stick it on your screen, or even whisper it to yourself. This simple step aligns your mind with your goal, making it harder for distractions to steal your attention.

Section 7: Make it a Game

Turning your work into a game can make focusing fun! Challenge yourself to complete a task before a certain song ends or beat your previous record. Our brains love a good challenge, and this playful approach can boost your determination to stay on track.

Section 8: Celebrate Small Wins

Acknowledge your victories, no matter how small. Completing a section of your task? Treat yourself to a quick stretch or a sip of your favorite drink. Celebrating small wins creates positive associations with focused work, making you more likely to stay in the zone.

Section 9: Fuel Your Focus with Proper Nutrition

Believe it or not, your diet plays a role in your ability to focus. Foods rich in omega-3 fatty acids, antioxidants, and vitamins can enhance brain function. Snack on nuts, blueberries, or dark chocolate during your work breaks to give your brain the boost it deserves.

Section 10: The Joy of JOMO (Joy of Missing Out)

In a world obsessed with FOMO (Fear of Missing Out), embrace JOMO – the Joy of Missing Out. Understand that by saying no to distractions, you're saying yes to accomplishing your goals and nurturing your growth. Embrace the joy that comes with being fully present and engaged in your work.

Congratulations! You've just leveled up your focus game. Remember, staying focused is a skill that takes practice. Be patient with yourself and keep implementing these strategies. Soon enough, you'll find yourself effortlessly zoning in on your tasks, conquering distractions, and achieving more than you ever thought possible.

Now, let's dive back into the action and conquer those tasks like the focused superstar you are!

Identifying Common Distractions and Their Impact on Your Progress

Distractions – those sneaky little things that pull us away from our goals and keep us from making meaningful progress. We've all been there, caught in the clutches of distractions, wondering where all our time went. But fear not, my friend! In this chapter, we'll dive deep into the world of distractions, understanding their various forms, and most importantly, learning how to wrangle them and regain control over our precious time.

The Distraction Dilemma: A Sneaky Saboteur

Distractions come in many forms, often lurking in plain sight. The allure of social media, the ping of incoming messages, the temptation of binge-watching your favorite show – these are just a few of the culprits that can lead us astray. They may seem harmless, but their impact on your progress is more significant than you might think.

Distraction Impact 101: Derailing Your Productivity Train

Distractions aren't just innocent time-wasters; they can have a profound effect on your overall productivity. Imagine you're working on an important project. You're in the zone, making steady progress, and suddenly, ding – an email notification grabs your attention. You switch tabs to check it out, and before you know it, you've lost track of time and your focus is shattered. Getting back to that productive state takes time, leaving you feeling frustrated and overwhelmed.

Identifying the Usual Suspects: Types of Distractions

Let's identify some of the common culprits that derail your progress:

Digital Dalliances: Social media, email, notifications – the digital world is full of traps. They seem harmless, but they can lead you down a rabbit hole of endless scrolling and clicking.

Chatty Cathy: Colleagues or friends who drop by for a quick chat can unknowingly consume a significant chunk of your time.

Multitasking Mayhem: Trying to juggle multiple tasks simultaneously might seem impressive, but it often results in reduced efficiency and quality.

Environmental Emissaries: Noise, clutter, and a disorganized workspace can chip away at your focus and disrupt your flow.

Taking Action: Decluttering Your Path to Progress

Now that we've identified the distractions, it's time to take action. Here's a simple and friendly approach to tackle distractions head-on:

Distraction Diary: Keep a journal for a few days to track your distractions. Note down what pulls you away from your tasks and how long you spend on each distraction.

Digital Detox: Set specific times for checking emails and social media. Use apps that block distracting websites during your work periods.

Time Blocking: Divide your day into chunks and allocate specific tasks to each block. Stick to the plan and avoid switching between tasks.

Declutter Your Space: Organize your workspace, keeping only what you need within arm's reach. A tidy environment promotes a clear mind.

Learn to Say No: Politely decline non-urgent interruptions and set boundaries to protect your focused time.

Mindful Breaks: Take regular breaks to recharge, but use them wisely. Step away from screens and engage in activities that truly refresh you.

Remember, progress is a series of small steps. By identifying and taming distractions, you're freeing up valuable time and energy to invest in what truly matters. So, go ahead, put on your distraction-blocking cape, and take charge of your journey toward remarkable progress!

Mindfulness and Concentration Exercises to Enhance Focus

In this chapter, we're diving into the magical world of mindfulness and concentration – two powerful tools that can supercharge your ability to focus like never before. In our fast-paced, always-connected lives, cultivating mindfulness and honing your concentration skills can be your secret weapons for staying on track and achieving your goals.

The Art of Mindfulness
Imagine being fully present in each moment, free from the distractions of the past and worries about the future. That's the essence of mindfulness – a

State of awareness that allows you to engage with your current task or experience wholeheartedly. Here's how to infuse mindfulness into your daily routine:

Mindful Breathing
Find a Quiet Space: Sit or lie down in a comfortable position in a quiet place where you won't be disturbed.

Focus on Your Breath: Close your eyes and turn your attention to your breath. Feel the sensation of the air entering and leaving your body.

Stay Present: As you breathe, thoughts might drift in. That's okay! Acknowledge them without judgment and gently guide your focus back to your breath.

Start Small: Begin with just a few minutes of mindful breathing each day, gradually extending the duration as you become more comfortable.

Mindful Observation
Choose an Object: Select an everyday object, like a piece of fruit or a flower.

Engage Your Senses: Examine the object closely, using all your senses. Notice its color, texture, scent, and any sounds associated with it.

Stay Curious: Approach the object with a sense of curiosity, as if you're seeing it for the first time. Let go of preconceived notions.

Expand Awareness: Try applying this practice to other aspects of your life, such as your surroundings during a walk or the taste of your meals.

Sharpening Your Concentration
Now that you're cultivating mindfulness, let's channel that focus into enhancing your concentration skills. The ability to concentrate deeply on a single task is like a mental muscle – the more you exercise it, the stronger it becomes.

The Pomodoro Technique
Set a Timer: Choose a task you want to focus on and set a timer for 25 minutes.

Work Intensely: During these 25 minutes, give your full attention to the task. Resist the urge to check your phone or get sidetracked.

Take a Break: After the 25 minutes, take a 5-minute break. Stretch, walk around, or simply relax.

Repeat: Repeat this cycle (called a "pomodoro") three times, then take a longer break of 15-30 minutes.

Single-Tasking
Prioritize One Task: Instead of juggling multiple tasks, commit to working on one task at a time.

Eliminate Distractions: Clear your workspace of any distractions – put away your phone, close unnecessary tabs, and create a clutter-free zone.

Set a Time Limit: Decide on a specific amount of time you'll dedicate to the task, such as 45 minutes.

Immerse Yourself: Fully engage with the task. If your mind starts to wander, gently guide it back to the task at hand.

By practicing mindfulness and concentration exercises regularly, you'll find your ability to focus and accomplish tasks greatly improved. Remember, it's a journey, so be patient with yourself. With time

And consistent effort, you'll develop a focused and calm mind that's ready to tackle any challenge that comes your way.

Designing an Environment for Laser-Focused Attention

Creating a space that helps you concentrate and stay on track doesn't require a complete overhaul. By making a few thoughtful adjustments, you can design an environment that supports your undivided attention and boosts your productivity. Let's dive into some simple yet effective steps to achieve this.

1. Declutter Your Space: A Clear Mind Starts with a Clear Desk
Imagine walking into a room with piles of papers and a cluttered desk. It can feel overwhelming and distract your focus. Start by decluttering your workspace. Keep only the essentials on your desk and find organized storage solutions for everything else.

2. Optimize Lighting: Let There Be Natural Light
Natural light has a positive impact on your mood and focus. Position your workspace near a window

To allow ample sunlight. If that's not possible, choose warm, white LED lights that mimic natural daylight. Avoid harsh fluorescent lighting that can strain your eyes.

3. Ergonomic Setup: Comfort and Productivity Hand in Hand

An uncomfortable chair or a poorly positioned monitor can lead to discomfort and distractions. Invest in an ergonomic chair and ensure your computer screen is at eye level. Your keyboard and mouse should be at a comfortable height to prevent strain.

4. Noise Management: Find Your Sound Sweet Spot

While complete silence may not work for everyone, excessive noise can disrupt your focus. Experiment with different noise levels to find what suits you best. Some people thrive with gentle background music or white noise, while others prefer total silence. Noise-canceling headphones can also be a game-changer.

5. Digital Detox: Taming the Technology Temptation

Your digital devices can be both a tool and a distraction. Use apps or browser extensions to block distracting websites or social media during focused work sessions. Designate specific times for checking emails and messages to prevent constant interruptions.

6. Personalize Your Space: Surround Yourself with Inspiration
Decorate your workspace with items that motivate and inspire you. Whether it's quotes, artwork, or photos of loved ones, these personal touches can create a positive and uplifting atmosphere.

7. Mindful Color Choices: Harnessing the Psychology of Colors
Colors can influence your mood and cognitive functions. Opt for colors that promote focus and creativity, such as calming blues or invigorating greens. Avoid overly bright or distracting colors that might disrupt your concentration.

8. Organizational Tools: Structure Breeds Efficiency
Use tools like calendars, planners, and to-do lists to keep yourself organized. Write down tasks and deadlines, and break them into manageable steps.

This visual structure can help you stay on track and feel a sense of accomplishment as you complete each task.

9. Create Zones: Divide and Conquer

If your space allows, create designated zones for different activities. Have a focused work area, a relaxation corner, and perhaps a place for quick brainstorming sessions. This division can help you mentally switch between tasks and maintain your attention.

10. Plants and Nature: A Breath of Fresh Air

Bringing a touch of nature indoors can enhance your environment. Plants not only improve air quality but also create a soothing ambiance. Choose low-maintenance plants that thrive indoors, and place them strategically around your workspace.

Remember, designing an attention-supportive environment is a personal journey. Experiment with these ideas and adapt them to your preferences. The goal is to create a space that resonates with you, fuels your motivation, and empowers you to achieve your goals with unwavering focus. So, go ahead and

Start transforming your surroundings into a haven for undivided attention and remarkable productivity!

Chapter 7
The Habit Loop: Cultivating Action-Taking Habits

Welcome to Chapter 7 of our exciting journey in "Get Things Done: The Action Taker's Guide to Overcoming Excuses." Here, we're digging into a powerful idea that can change your ability to take action and achieve your goals – the Habit Loop.

Think of the Habit Loop as your unique tool for getting things done. It's like having a trusty friend that leads you easily toward your goals. So, let's break it down in the easiest and nicest way possible.

Step 1: The Cue – Sparking the Action

Imagine you're going out on a goal, whether it's hitting the gym, working on a project, or learning a new skill. Every action starts with a cue – a little nudge that tells your brain to get into gear. Cues can be anything – a specific time of day, a place, a feeling, or even an event. The magic lies in finding cues that match with your goals.

Friendly Tip: Choose cues that easily fit into your pattern. For instance, if you want to exercise more, set your sneakers right by the door as a visible sign. Or if you're trying to read more, place a book on your desk.

Step 2: The Routine – Taking Action

Now comes the fun part – the routine! This is where you dive into action. Let's say your cue is getting home from work. You change into your workout clothes and head to the gym. The key here is to keep the practice easy and doable. The easier it is, the more likely you are to stick with it.

Friendly Tip: Start small. If your goal is to relax everyday, begin with just a couple of minutes and gradually increase the time as it becomes a habit.

Step 3: The Reward – Celebrating Your Victory

Ah, the prize – your brain's way of saying, "Great job, you did it!" This could be a sense of success, a feeling of joy, or even a treat you give yourself. The reward strengthens your brain's link between the cue

And the routine, making it more likely that you'll repeat the action in the future.

Friendly Tip: Make the prize important to you. It could be as simple as checking off a to-do list item or treating yourself to a bit of dark chocolate.

Step 4: The Loop – Repetition Is Key

Here's where the magic happens. By constantly following this cue-routine-reward loop, you're building a habit. Over time, your brain starts to crave the pattern because it associates it with a good payoff. And voilà, taking action becomes second nature!

Friendly Tip: Be patient. Habits take time to solidify. Experts say it might take around 66 days on average for a new behavior to become routine.

Step 5: Tweaking and Growing

As you start on your action-taking habit journey, remember that freedom is your friend. Life is dynamic, and sometimes your cues or habits might

Need a little change. That's totally okay! The goal is growth, not perfection.

Friendly Tip: When life throws a surprise, change your practice instead of giving up. If you miss a day, don't stress – just get back on track the next day.

So, dear Action Taker, welcome the Habit Loop with open arms. It's your secret tool to easily weave action-taking into your daily life. Soon, you'll find yourself finishing tasks, meeting goals, and thinking how you ever lived without this amazing tool.

Now, take a moment to think on the cues that could kickstart your action-taking journey. Remember, small regular steps lead to big results. Get ready to level up your life – one action-taking habit at a time!

Understanding the Science of Habit Formation and Its Role in Success

Imagine if meeting your goals and getting success could be as easy as putting on your best pair of shoes every morning. Well, the study of habit creation says that it's possible! Habits are like those well-worn tracks in a forest that you easily follow –

They guide your actions without much conscious effort. In this chapter, we're going to dive into the interesting world of habit development and how it can be your secret tool on the journey to success.

What Are Habits and How Do They Form?

Habits are like your brain's tools to get things done. When you regularly do an action in a certain situation, your brain starts to build a thought link between the action and the context. It's like making a bridge between neurons – the more you cross it, the stronger it becomes.

Let's say you want to start a daily workout program. At first, it might feel like a chore, but if you stick to it, your brain starts associating exercise with, let's say, wearing workout clothes. Over time, the simple sight of those clothes prompts the desire to exercise. Voila! You've made a habit.

The Habit Loop: Cue, Routine, Reward

Habits have a framework called the Habit Loop – it's like a three-step dance that happens in your brain:

Cue: This is the trigger that kicks off the habit. It could be a specific time of day, a feeling, or an event. In the workout case, your cue might be finishing work for the day.

Routine: This is the action you take in reaction to the cue. Going for a jog or hitting the gym, in our case.

Reward: The best part! This is what your brain looks forward to. It could be the sense of success, the rush of endorphins after exercise, or even a tasty protein shake.

Hacking the Habit Loop for Success

Now, let's talk about how you can use this Habit Loop to your advantage:

Choose a Keystone Habit: Some habits have a domino effect, positively affecting other parts of your life. These are called core habits. For instance, regular exercise often leads to better eating habits and improved attention.

Start Small: Remember, you're not running a race on day one. Make your desired action so small that it feels almost easy. Want to read more? Start with one page a day.

Be Consistent: Consistency is the magic element. Try to do your chosen deed at the same time and in the same setting every day. It helps strengthen the habit loop.

Celebrate Your Wins: Don't underestimate the power of a little party. Acknowledge your growth and pat yourself on the back. This increases the reward part of the habit loop.

Stay Patient: Habits don't form overnight. Research says it takes about 66 days, on average, to develop a new habit. So, be patient and keep at it.

Habits and Your Path to Success

Now, you might be thinking, how does all this habit stuff lead to success? Well, imagine if you had a set of habits that automatically led you toward your goals. Want to become a better writer? Imagine having a habit of writing a page every morning.

Dream of being more organized? Picture a habit of cleaning for just 5 minutes every evening.

Habits make success feel less like an overwhelming climb and more like a set of fun steps. They free up your brain energy because you're not constantly arguing whether or not to take action – you just do it.

So, as you start on your road to success, remember that habits can be your reliable partners. They can help you reach your goals with less work and more fun. So go ahead, lace up those habit shoes, and start your dance towards success!

Replacing Old Habits with Productive Action-Taking Routines: Your Guide to Positive Change

We all have habits – those little routines that shape our days. Some habits boost us, while others hold us back. If you've been wanting to break free from old habits and accept new, action-taking routines, you're in the right place. In this guide, we're going to walk you through the process step by step, in a nice and Simple way, to help you start on a journey of positive change.

Step 1: Self-Discovery and Awareness

First things first, take a moment to think on your present habits. Which ones are helping you grow, and which ones are hurting your progress? Be gentle with yourself – this is a judgment-free zone. Identify the habits you wish to change, and set your goal to build new, effective ones.

Step 2: Define Your Vision

Imagine your perfect day – full of successes, joy, and satisfaction. What steps would you take to make that day a reality? Visualize yourself as the Action Taker you strive to be. This goal will be your guide light as you create new habits.

Step 3: Start Small and Be Specific

Big changes often begin with small steps. Choose one habit to focus on improving originally. Make it specific – instead of saying "I'll exercise more," say "I'll walk for 15 minutes every morning." Specificity makes your goal real and doable.

Step 4: Create Triggers

Link your new action-taking pattern to a current habit. For instance, if you're trying to read more, place a book next to your morning coffee. Your morning coffee becomes the spark for your reading habit. This relationship helps the new habit stick.

Step 5: Celebrate Progress

Celebrate every win, no matter how small. Did you successfully adopt your new plan for a week? Treat yourself to something you enjoy – a movie night, a favorite snack, or a relaxing bath. Positive feedback increases your determination.

Step 6: Stay Consistent

Consistency is key. As you combine your new schedule into your daily life, be patient with yourself. It takes time for a habit to become second nature. Set notes, use schedules, or even find an accountability partner to help you stay on track.

Step 7: Adjust and Adapt

Life is changeable, and so are your habits. If you hit a roadblock or your practice isn't quite fitting in, don't give up. Instead, adapt. Modify the routine to better fit your plan and tastes. The goal is growth, not perfection.

Step 8: Practice Mindfulness

During your new action-taking practice, be present. Feel the feelings, emotions, and thoughts that come. Mindfulness improves the experience and strengthens the habit loop in your brain.

Step 9: Embrace Setbacks as Learning Opportunities

Encountered a setback? Don't be worried. Setbacks are normal parts of change. Reflect on what led to the loss and how you can beat similar challenges in the future. Each failure is a chance to learn and grow.

Step 10: Build Momentum

Once your first new habit is established, gradually add more action-taking routines. As you build confidence, you'll find it easier to change bad habits with good ones. Remember, you're on a journey of ongoing improvement.

In conclusion, changing old habits with effective action-taking routines is a process of self-discovery, patience, and determination. By following these steps in a friendly and simple way, you can change your daily life and become the Action Taker you imagine. Remember, you have the power to shape your habits and, in turn, shape your future. Start today and accept the good changes that await you!

Nurturing Habits That Feel Like Second Nature and Bring Lasting Results

Congratulations on starting on your journey to become an Action Taker! One of the most powerful tools at your hands is the ability to develop habits that become second nature. Imagine easily finishing jobs that once felt difficult, and consistently getting the results you desire. In this chapter, we'll dig into the art of growing habits that not only stick but also drive regular, positive results. So, let's dive in and Find the secrets to making lasting changes in the easiest and nicest way.

Step 1: Start Small and Specific

When it comes to building habits, it's important to start small. Choose a specific action that you want to turn into a habit. Whether it's exercise for 10 minutes a day or reading a few pages of a book, find a doable job that you can easily work into your routine. Remember, the goal is to make it so easy that you can't say no!

Step 2: Set a Trigger

Triggers are like gentle warnings that nudge you toward your desired action. They could be existing cues in your surroundings, like putting your workout clothes next to your bed or setting a daily alarm for your reading time. A trigger sends to your brain that it's time to engage in your chosen action.

Step 3: Be Consistent

Consistency is the magic factor that makes actions into habits. Aim to perform your chosen action at The same time or in the same setting every day. Whether it's right after you wake up, during your lunch break, or before bed, find a slot that works for you and stick to it. The more constant you are, the more your brain will wire itself to expect and accept the exercise.

Step 4: Celebrate Small Wins

Every time you successfully finish your chosen move, celebrate! It could be as easy as a fist pump, a smile, or a thought pat on the back. Celebrating your wins, no matter how small, releases feel-good chemicals in your brain, strengthening the habit loop and making you more likely to repeat the action.

Step 5: Stay Patient and Positive

Remember, building habits takes time. Be patient with yourself and don't get frustrated if you miss a day or face hurdles. Instead of focusing on failures, focus on the progress you've made and the positive effect your habit is having on your life. Cultivate an attitude of self-compassion and resilience.

Step 6: Adjust and Evolve
As you get comfortable with your starting habit, don't be afraid to level up. You can gradually increase the volume or length of your chosen move.

Alternatively, you can introduce new habits that match with your goals. The key is to keep changing while ensuring the habits remain doable and fun.

By following these simple steps and filling them with a friendly, understanding attitude, you'll find yourself easily accepting habits that drive consistent results. Before you know it, you'll look forward to these actions as an important part of your daily routine. With time, they'll become second nature, pushing you toward your goals and changing you into a true Action Taker. So, get started, be kind to yourself, and let the path of developing powerful habits begin!

Chapter 8
The Power of Accountability and Support

Welcome to Chapter 8 of 'Get Things Done,' where we'll study a game-changing idea that can boost your action-taking journey: The Power of Accountability and Support. Picture this chapter as your trusty co-pilot, leading you through the air of work with a friendly voice and a strong plan.

Section 1: The Accountability Advantage

Accountability isn't about pointing fingers or putting blame. It's like having a trusted friend who cheers you on and gently nudges you forward. When you share your goals and plans with someone, it causes a strong psychological affect. Suddenly, your promises are no longer whispers in the wind; they're vows made to yourself and others.

In this part, we'll look into: The Accountability Partner: Finding that person who'll have your back and hold you to your word.

Clear Expectations: How to set up effective responsibility plans that keep you driven.

Regular Check-Ins: The art of steady progress reports and enjoying small wins together.

Section 2: Building a Supportive Network

Life's journey is often smoother with partners. Surrounding yourself with like-minded individuals who share your desire for action-taking can be a game-changer. This part is all about building your "Action Team":

Finding Your Tribe: Identifying people who agree with your goals and ideals.
Positive Peer Pressure: How a helpful network can spark healthy competition and mutual growth.
Sharing Wisdom: Exchanging experiences and ideas for joint growth.
Section 3: Self-Accountability Techniques

While external responsibility is powerful, let's not forget your inner sense. In this area, we'll study methods to be your own best accountability partner:

Written Commitments: The magic of jotting down your promises and goals.
Visual Reminders: Creating visual cues that keep your goals front and center.
Reward Systems: Treating yourself for hitting goals – because you deserve it!
Section 4: The Ripple Effect of Accountability

Accountability isn't just about getting stuff done; it has a ripple effect on your life. It boosts your self-esteem, improves your relationships, and cultivates a feeling of duty. This part unpacks:

Increased Confidence: How completing your obligations boosts your self-confidence.
Enhanced Relationships: The effect of being reliable and trustworthy in your relationships.
Becoming a Role Model: Inspiring others through your commitment to action-taking.
Section 5: Accountability Challenges and Solutions

Nothing worth having comes easy, right? In this part, we'll cover common obstacles and useful solutions:

Slipping Up: How to bounce back from failures and keep responsibility.
Accountability Fatigue: Dealing with burnout and renewing your resolve.
Navigating Differences: Handling arguments or different methods within your support network.
Remember, responsibility and support are your secret tools in the fight against delay and excuses.

This chapter will give you with a set of skills and a warm community that will keep you on track, even when the going gets tough.

So, are you ready to join forces with your accountability partners and take your action-taking journey to new heights? Let's dive in and accept the power of responsibility and support together!

Harnessing the Power of Accountability Partners and Mentors: Your Path to Achieving Goals Together

Are you ready to boost your road towards success? One of the most effective and fun ways to achieve your goals is by getting the support of accountability partners and teachers. These amazing people can provide you with the advice, motivation, and support you need to take action and make your dreams a reality. In this chapter, we'll dive deep into the world of accountability partnerships and coaching, Studying how you can leverage these relationships to turbocharge your progress.

Understanding Accountability Partnerships:

Picture this: You're on a road trip with a close friend. You're both following the same road, sharing stories, and helping each other beat hurdles along the way. An accountability partnership works in a similar way. It's a joint pledge between you and another person to support each other's goals. Whether you're trying to finish a project, adopt a better lifestyle, or start a new business venture, having an accountability partner can make a world of difference.

Finding the Right Accountability Partner:

Choosing the right responsibility partner is important. Look for someone who shares your ideals, knows your goals, and is committed to their own growth as well. This journey is about mutual support, so it's important to pick someone with whom you feel safe sharing your achievements, failures, and difficulties.

Setting Clear Goals and Expectations:

Once you've found your accountability partner, it's time to set clear goals and standards. Define what you both want to achieve and create a plan to track progress. This could involve regular check-ins, goal-setting meetings, or even joint projects. The key is to keep each other on track and hold each other responsible in a nice and non-judgmental way.

The Role of Mentors:

While accountability partners work alongside you as friends, teachers are experienced guides who offer knowledge, insights, and advice based on their own journeys. A guide can provide a wider viewpoint, helping you handle obstacles and chances you might not have considered. Think of them as your personal supporters, always ready to share their knowledge and provide advice.

Finding Your Mentor:

When finding a guide, look for someone who has achieved what you desire to accomplish. Their knowledge and experience will be essential as you Try to take action and reach your goals. Don't be afraid to approach possible teachers; many successful individuals are eager to give back and help others on their paths to success.

Nurturing the Mentor-Mentee Relationship:

Building a good mentor-mentee connection takes clear conversation, respect, and a desire to learn. Be prepared to ask questions, seek help, and listen carefully to your mentor's observations. Remember, their advice is a gift, and your excitement and commitment will be a testament to their investment in your growth.

Fostering a Supportive Community:

Accountability partners and teachers can form the basis of a caring community that uplifts and supports each other. Participate in group talks, classes, and networking events to meet with like-minded people who are also taking action towards their goals. Sharing stories and learning from others can improve your trip and provide a sense of unity.

Celebrating Progress Together:

As you make steps towards your goals, don't forget to enjoy your successes, both big and small, with your accountability partner, instructor, and the community. Acknowledging your wins boosts mood and pushes you to keep going forward. Plus, sharing your wins with your support network improves the joy of success.

Embracing the Journey:

In the world of accountability relationships and guidance, taking action becomes a shared journey. By working with a trusted partner and learning from experienced teachers, you'll find yourself more inspired, driven, and equipped to conquer hurdles and take opportunities. So, why go it alone when you can start on this exciting journey with friends who truly care about your success?

Remember, it's not just about getting the goal; it's about enjoying every step of the action-taking trip together. Embrace the power of responsibility partnerships and teachers, and watch as your dreams Come to life in ways you never thought possible. Your success story starts now!

Building a Supportive Network that Energizes Your Action-Taking Journey

Embarking on your action-taking trip is an exciting adventure, but it's important to remember that you don't have to go it alone. One of the most valuable tools you can have by your side is a helpful network that cheers you on, offers advice, and holds you responsible. Imagine having a group of friends who are like your personal fans, pulling for you every step of the way. Let's look into how you can build and develop this powerful support system.

1. Identify Your Allies:
Start by finding the people in your life who truly support your goals and ambitions. These could be friends, family members, peers, teachers, or even online groups. Look for individuals who share your beliefs, understand your journey, and are truly excited about your progress.

2. Share Your Vision:
Openly share your goals and action plans with your chosen partners. Sharing your vision with others not only strengthens your commitment but also helps them to understand how they can best support you. When they know what you're working towards, they can offer customized help and support.

3. Seek Guidance:

Don't hesitate to reach out to those who have taken a similar road or achieved similar goals. Their thoughts and experiences can provide priceless advice. Ask questions, seek help, and learn from their achievements and obstacles. Remember, most people are pleased to be asked for advice and are happy to help.

4. Accountability Partners:

Pair up with an accountability person who is also trying to achieve their own goals. This joint support system creates a sense of duty. Regular check-ins with your partner keep you on track and encouraged. Share your progress, celebrate each other's wins, and offer helpful comments when required.

5. Encourage Each Other:

Within your supporting network, create an environment of positive feedback. Celebrate even the tiny wins and achievements. A simple "You've got this!" or "I believe in you!" from a friend can provide the boost of inspiration you need to keep moving forward.

6. Attend Workshops and Meetups:

Consider taking classes, lectures, and meetups connected to your job or hobbies. These events provide chances to meet with like-minded people who are also excited about taking action. You'll learn new skills, gain fresh views, and grow your network in the process.

7. Online Communities:

In the digital age, internet groups offer a wealth of support and connection. Join communities, Facebook groups, or sites focused on your goals. Engage in conversations, ask questions, and share your progress. These groups often provide a safe space to seek help and support.

8. Be a Giver:

Remember, a helpful network is a two-way street. Be ready to offer your help and guidance to others As well. By being a good force in someone else's journey, you create a ripple effect of drive and inspiration.

9. Embrace Diversity:

Your supporting network doesn't have to consist only of people with the same goals. Diversity in views and experiences can improve your trip.

Engaging with people from different backgrounds can provide fresh ideas and answers you might not have considered.

10. Stay Connected and Express Gratitude:
Nurture your network by staying linked and showing thanks. Regularly inform your friends on your progress, difficulties, and wins. A simple thank-you note or act of praise goes a long way in keeping strong relationships.

Remember, building a supporting network takes time and effort, but the benefits are immeasurable. Surrounding yourself with individuals who boost and encourage you changes your action-taking path into a shared adventure. Together, you can conquer obstacles, enjoy wins, and build a lively community that drives your progress. So, reach out, connect, And watch as your journey becomes even more lively with the support of your discovered friends.

Techniques for Holding Yourself and Others Responsible for Commitments

Accountability is the cornerstone of successful action-taking. It's not just about planning to do something – it's about ensuring that those promises translate into real results. Whether you're working individually or within a friendly team, learning the art of responsibility can make a world of difference in meeting your goals. In this part, we'll explore practical and reasonable techniques to hold yourself and others responsible for promises in a simple and nice way.

1. Clear Communication and Expectations:
Begin by setting crystal-clear goals. When making promises, describe the details of what needs to be achieved, by when, and the desired results. Similarly, when engaging others, ensure that everyone knows their jobs and duties. Effective communication leaves no room for misunderstanding, making it easier to track progress and hold everyone responsible.
2. SMART Goals:
Adopt the SMART (Specific, Measurable, Achievable, Relevant, Time-bound) approach for setting goals and obligations. Break down bigger jobs into smaller, doable steps, each with its own limit. This not only avoids overwhelm but also gives regular goals for review and responsibility.

3. Regular Check-Ins:
Frequent check-ins provide chances to review work and make necessary changes. Whether it's a weekly team meeting or a personal review, share what's been accomplished, any difficulties faced, and the plan for going forward. These check-ins promote a sense of duty and open dialogue.

4. Positive Reinforcement:
Celebrate successes, no matter how small. Positive feedback produces a motivating setting and supports constant effort. Acknowledging success, giving praise, or even small prizes can boost mood and strengthen the resolve to taking action.

5. Empowerment and Ownership:
Give people the authority to take ownership of their obligations. When people feel powerful, they are More likely to hold themselves responsible. Encourage team members to take initiative, make choices, and add their unique skills to the project.

6. Peer Accountability Partners:
Pair up team members as responsibility partners. This develops a supporting system where people hold each other responsible for their promises.

Regular check-ins between partners create a sense of friendship and a shared commitment to success.

7. Visual Aids and Progress Tracking:
Visual tools, such as progress charts or project boards, provide a physical picture of promises and their state. Seeing jobs move from "to-do" to "done" can be incredibly inspiring. Make it a joint effort by involving the team in changing these images.

8. Constructive Feedback:
Feedback should be a two-way process. Offer helpful comments when promises aren't met, focused on answers rather than blame. Encourage open talks about obstacles and explore ways to solve them together.

9. Flexibility and Adaptability:
Life is uncertain, and sometimes unplanned events can affect our ability to meet obligations. Foster a culture of understanding and flexibility, allowing for changes while keeping a strong commitment to the end goal.

10. Lead by Example:

Whether you're a team boss or an individual worker, leading by example is powerful. Demonstrate your loyalty to tasks, goals, and quality work. Your acts will inspire others to do the same.

In conclusion, responsibility is not about putting pressure or causing fear, but rather about building an environment where promises are respected and action is taken with excitement. By applying these techniques, you'll create a mindset of responsibility, trust, and cooperation that drives everyone towards success. Remember, it's not just about holding others responsible – it's about collectively accepting a journey of growth and success.

Chapter 9
Conquering Fear and Stepping into Growth

Fear – it's that annoying voice in your head that whispers doubts, feeds fears, and stops you from taking the jumps you need to grow. But guess what? You have the power to flip the script and use fear as a spring to bounce into growth. In this chapter, we're diving deep into the world of fear, and we're going to give you with simple, friendly tools to beat it and step boldly into the realm of personal and professional growth.

1. Embrace Your Fear:
Fear isn't the enemy; it's a sign that you're onto something big. Imagine a roller coaster – that mix of joy and fear before the drop. That's fear telling you that you're about to experience something exciting. So, instead of shying away from fear, accept it. It's a sign that you're going beyond your comfort zone and aiming for something special.

2. Reframe Failure:
Fear often stems from a fear of failing. But what if we told you that loss is your friend? Every great person has a run of mistakes behind them, each one A lesson that pushed them forward. Embrace loss as a necessary step toward growth. Celebrate your tries, and if things don't go as planned, take it as a badge of honor that you had the guts to try.

3. Start Small:

Taking a giant leap into the unknown can be frightening. Instead, start with tiny steps. It's like starting to swim – you dip your toes before jumping in. Break down your big goal into smaller, doable jobs. Each small success will boost your confidence and help you build momentum, making the big leap feel less scary.

4. The Power of Visualization:
Visualization is your secret tool against fear. Close your eyes and truly imagine yourself succeeding. Feel the excitement, the pride, and the joy of reaching your goal. When fear creeps in, remember this mental picture. It'll tell you of your potential and change your attention from fear to opportunity.

5. Surround Yourself with Positivity:
Ever noticed how criticism feeds fear? Surround yourself with positive forces – friends, teachers, books, talks – that boost and support you. When fear Tries to come in, these factors will be your cheerleaders, telling you of your powers and pushing you to take action.

6. Embrace the Unknown:

Growth happens outside your safe zone. Instead of fearing the unknown, be interested about it. Treat every new event as a journey. What will you learn? How will you evolve? Approach the unknown with an open mind, and you'll find that fear loses its power.

7. Take Inspired Action:
Action based in inspiration is a fear-buster. When you're truly motivated by a goal or a dream, fear takes a place. Focus on the reason behind your action – the effect it'll have on your life or the lives of others. Let that energy lead you forward, and fear will find itself in the back row.

8. Cultivate Self-Compassion:
Fear often grows on self-criticism. Counter it with self-compassion. Treat yourself with the same kindness you'd give a friend. If things don't go as planned, don't beat yourself up. Instead, focus on what you've learned and how you can improve. This Gentle method reduces fear's power and boosts your resolve.

9. Learn and Evolve:

Every move you take, whether good or not, is a lesson. Embrace these lessons as chances for growth. Ask yourself what you've learned, how you've grown, and what you'll do differently next time. This mindset shift takes fear from a roadblock into a stepping stone.

10. Celebrate Your Courage:
Finally, celebrate every step you take to beat fear. Acknowledge your bravery. Treat yourself to something you love when you beat a fear block. Celebrating your courage repeats the message that fear is no match for your drive.

Remember, fear is just a passing cloud; growth is the sky that goes beyond it. By accepting fear and taking action despite it, you're not only moving into growth – you're flying into a world of unlimited opportunities. So, take a deep breath, take that step, and watch your world grow before your eyes.

Identifying and Overcoming Fear: Your Key to Taking Action

Fear – it's that tiny voice inside your head that whispers questions and what-ifs, the knot in your chest that holds you back, and the unseen barrier that stands between you and your dreams. We've all been there – faced with chances that seem tantalizingly out of reach due to fear. But guess what? You have the power to beat this fear and unlock your action-taking potential!

Understanding Fear:

Before we dive into beating fear, let's understand what it really is. Fear is a normal human reaction to the unknown or imagined dangers. It's your brain's way of trying to keep you safe. But sometimes, fear can become overprotective, stopping you from trying new things or taking risks. It's like a well-meaning friend who tells you against going out of your comfort zone.

Identifying Fear:

The first step is to notice fear when it rears its head. It might come dressed as reasons – "I'm not ready," "What if I fail?" – or it might appear physically as sweaty hands and a beating heart. Pay attention to these signs; they're telling you that fear is in play.

Name Your Fear:

Give your fear a name. It might sound silly, but this helps to separate yourself from the fear. For instance, if you're afraid of public speaking, you could call it "Stage Jitters." This simple act of naming makes it easier to address.

Analyze Your Fear:

Take a better look at your fear. What's the worst that could happen? What's the best that could happen? Often, you'll learn that the worst-case scenario isn't as terrible as your mind makes it out to be.

The Power of Visualization:

Close your eyes and imagine yourself defeating your fear. See yourself taking action, achieving, and feeling powerful. Visualization tricks your brain into Feeling like it's already achieved the job, making the real action seem less scary.

Overcoming Fear:

Now, let's face fear head-on and show it who's boss!

Break It Down:

Big, difficult goals can increase fear. Break your goal into smaller, doable steps. Each step you achieve chips away at your fear and builds your confidence.

Knowledge is Courage:

Educate yourself. Often, fear lives on misinformation. The more you know about what you're facing, the more sure you'll feel. Knowledge truly is power.

Embrace Failure:

Fear of failing is a biggie. But guess what? Failure is not the end – it's a starting stone. It's where you Learn, grow, and come back even better. Embracing defeat takes away its power to stop you.

Take Baby Steps:

Start small. If your fear is talking to strangers, begin by making small talk with someone at a social event.

Gradually work your way up. Each small step is a success.

Positive Affirmations:

Counteract fear with upbeat self-talk. Repeat affirmations like "I am capable," "I can do this," and "I am in control." Over time, these affirmations will drown out the voice of fear.

Seek Support:

Share your fear with a trusted friend or guide. Sometimes, talking about your fear out loud reduces its hold on you. Plus, they might have useful tips or support to offer.

Remember, conquering fear is a journey, not a race. Celebrate each victory, no matter how small. By Meeting your fears head-on and taking action despite them, you're not just beating your doubts – you're opening a world of options and growth.

So, take a deep breath, put on your action-taking superhero cape, and step boldly into the unknown.

Your ideas are waiting – and you've got what it takes to make them a reality!

Embracing Discomfort: Your Catalyst for Remarkable Growth

Have you ever felt that uncomfortable ache in your stomach when faced with a new challenge? Or perhaps you've paused to step out of your comfort zone because the idea of pain made you uneasy? It's time to rethink your viewpoint and see pain as the strong spark for growth that it truly is. In this chapter, we'll explore how you can accept discomfort and turn it into your friend on the path to amazing personal and professional growth.

The Comfort Zone Conundrum

Picture your comfort zone as a cozy bubble, a place where you're at ease and familiar with your Surroundings. While this bubble gives a sense of comfort, it can also be a barrier to growth. Growth doesn't occur in safety – it happens when you move beyond your known limits. So, the first step is admitting that real change takes place outside your comfort zone.

Redefining Discomfort

Discomfort doesn't have to mean anxiety or pain. Think of it as a sign that you're stretching yourself, like a muscle during a workout. Just as your muscles become stronger after training, you become mentally and emotionally stronger when you face pain head-on.

Start Small, but Start Today

You don't need to jump into the deep end of pain instantly. Begin with doable steps. If public speaking scares you, start by sharing your thoughts in a small, friendly group. Gradually, you'll build courage to speak to bigger groups. Remember, every small step forward is a win.

Shift Your Perspective on Failure
Discomfort often stems from the fear of loss. But here's the truth: failure is not the end, it's a moving stone. Embrace a growth attitude that sees loss as a useful lesson. Each mistake is a chance to learn, change, and come back better.

Set Bold Goals

Goals that push you and make you a bit uncomfortable are the ones that lead to serious growth. Aim higher than you think you can reach, and you'll surprise yourself with what you can achieve. Break these goals into smaller, doable steps, and handle them one by one.

Practice Resilience and Self-Compassion

Discomfort may bring failures, but perseverance is your shield. When things don't go as planned, view it as a chance to improve your method. And remember, be kind to yourself. Self-compassion in times of trouble helps you bounce back stronger.

Embrace Continuous Learning

Learning itself can be uncomfortable, especially when you're faced with new knowledge or skills. Embrace a love for learning and see each task as a chance to expand your knowledge and skills.

Surround Yourself with Support

Share your discomfort with trusted friends, teachers, or peers. You'll often find that others have faced similar difficulties and can offer advice or support. A helpful network can make pain feel less frightening.

Celebrate Your Progress

Acknowledge every step you take out of your comfort zone. Celebrate your bravery and growth. Whether it's a small success or a big milestone, these parties support the idea that pain leads to good results.

Reflect and Adjust

Regularly think on your trip. What discomforts have you accepted, and how have they added to your growth? Adjust your goals, tactics, and attitude Accordingly. This ongoing self-awareness ensures that you're always moving forward.

Remember, accepting discomfort isn't about seeking out pain; it's about seeking out challenges that push your limits and ignite your potential. It's a journey of constant growth. So, step out of your comfort zone, accept the pain, and watch yourself change into the best version of you. The pain you feel today will become the strength you hold tomorrow.

Welcome to the exciting world of continuous growth and self-improvement! In this chapter, we'll start on a journey that promises to change your attitude and release your potential through the power of constant learning and evolution. Get ready to accept an attitude that not only pushes you forward but makes each step of your action-taking adventure a delightful experience.

1. Embrace Curiosity as Your Guide:
Picture yourself as an eager student of knowledge, always trying to discover new insights. Cultivate an interest that drives your desire to learn and understand. Approach each day with a childlike wonder, asking questions and finding solutions. Remember, there's no limit to what you can find when interest takes the lead.

2. Be a Sponge, Not a Rock:
Imagine your mind as a sponge that happily soaks up information from every source. Engage with books, talks, classes, and people who question your

viewpoint. Absorb new ideas like a sponge takes water, allowing them to expand your views and change your thinking.

3. Embrace Mistakes as Stepping Stones:
Shift your viewpoint on mistakes. Instead of fearing them, view them as important stepping stones on your path to growth. Every mistake is a lesson in disguise, offering insights that push you further along your journey. Celebrate your mistakes as chances for learning and improvement.

4. Set Bite-Sized Learning Goals:
Break down your learning journey into small, doable steps. Set realistic goals that encourage constant growth. Rather than overwhelming yourself with massive chores, focus on small changes that build over time. Celebrate each success, no matter how small, as a win.

5. Embrace Lifelong Learning:
Recognize that learning is not limited to traditional schooling. Embrace the idea of ongoing learning, where each day is a chance to grow your knowledge. Whether you're discovering a new hobby, gaining a skill, or increasing your understanding of a subject,

approach each experience with an open mind and a thirst for growth.

6. Surround Yourself with Growth-Minded Individuals:

Connect with like-minded people who share your desire for constant learning. Engage in talks that spark intellectual interest and challenge you to discover new paths. Collaborate, trade ideas, and learn from one another's experiences. A helpful group can increase your development.

7. Reflect and Adapt:

Regularly stop to think on your learning journey. What have you discovered? How have you evolved? Assess your work and make changes as needed. Adapt your goals and strategies based on your fresh insights, ensuring that your path stays connected with your ambitions.

8. Embrace Failure as Feedback:

Release the fear of loss and view it as priceless feedback. Each loss offers views into areas that require growth and improvement. Embrace the lessons loss offers and use them to improve your approach. Remember, every successful person has faced loss on their journey to greatness.

9. Celebrate Your Wins:
Acknowledge and enjoy your successes, no matter how small they may seem. Each milestone met is a proof to your commitment and growth. Reward yourself for your efforts, encouraging the positive loop of learning, action, and joy.

10. Share Your Knowledge:
Pay it forward by sharing your gained information and experiences with others. Teaching strengthens your learning and helps you to add to the growth of those around you. As you help others on their learning journeys, you'll find yourself changing even further.

Congratulations, you're now prepared with the tools to develop an attitude of constant learning and growth. Embrace each day as a chance to expand Your horizons, adapt to new obstacles, and change into the best version of yourself. Let your ravenous curiosity and dedication to growth lead the way, and watch as the world becomes your school and life itself a work of constant improvement.

Chapter 10
Celebrating Wins and Sustaining Momentum

Welcome to the final chapter of our journey together in "Get Things Done: The Action Taker's Guide to

Overcoming Excuses." In this chapter, we'll dive into the exciting world of celebrating your accomplishments and keeping that energy running as you continue your path of action and achievement.

Embrace Your Victories: The Importance of Celebration

Picture this: You've been carefully working on your goals, beating hurdles, and taking constant action. It's important to stop and recognize your success. Celebrating your wins isn't just a fun activity; it's a powerful tool for your growth and drive. When you party, you're telling yourself, "Hey, I did it!" This boosts your self-confidence, supports good behaviors, and fires your desire to accomplish even more.

How to Celebrate in Style

Celebrations don't have to be big or expensive; they can be as simple as treating yourself to your favorite meal, taking a day off to rest, or sharing your success with a close friend. The key is to make it important to you. Here's how you can enjoy your wins:

focus and Appreciate: Take a moment to focus on your successes. Recognize the work, time, and commitment you've spent. This self-appreciation lays the basis for real joy.

Set Milestone Rewards: Break your bigger goals into smaller steps. Assign prizes for hitting these goals. It could be anything from a movie night to getting that book you've been eyeing.

Share the Joy: Share your successes with friends, family, or a caring group. Their cheers and support increase your happiness and inspire you to keep going.

Capture the Moment: Take pictures, write about your success, or make a visual representation of Your trip. These lessons serve as motivation during difficult times.

Pamper Yourself: Treat yourself to something you love. It could be a spa day, a new tool, or a nice evening in. The act of treating yourself strengthens the good feelings connected with your success.

Sustaining Momentum for Ongoing Success

Celebrating wins isn't just a one-time event; it's a habit that pushes you forward. It produces a good feedback process that feeds your desire. But how do you maintain this momentum? Let's break it down:

Set New Goals: As you enjoy one success, put that energy into making new, interesting goals. Having a clear picture of what's next keeps you focused and excited.

Learn and Adapt: Take time to examine what worked well and what could be better in your recent effort. Apply these lessons to your future activities.

Consistency is Key: Keep up the constant action-taking habits you've developed. Momentum lives on regularity, so stay committed to your habits.

Surround Yourself with Positivity: Surround yourself with people who boost and support you.

Positive forces make it easier to stay inspired and continue celebrating together.

Visualize Your Future: Regularly visualize your future success. Imagine the feeling of achieving your goals. This mental practice keeps your drive high and your attention sharp.

Remember, celebrating wins isn't about flaunting your achievements; it's about honoring your progress and nurturing a mindset of success. By celebrating and sustaining momentum, you're creating a cycle of growth, accomplishment, and continuous improvement.

As we wrap up "Get Things Done," I encourage you to take these lessons to heart. Become the master of action-taking, banish excuses, and cultivate a life filled with purpose and achievement. You've got this! Here's to your ongoing success and the Remarkable journey that lies ahead. Cheers to you, the ultimate Action Taker!

Ready to celebrate your wins and keep the momentum going? Start by setting your next exciting goal and planning your well-deserved celebration. Your journey of action and achievement continues!

The Journey of Success: Celebrating Your Wins Along the Way

Hey there, fellow Action Taker! Let's dive into a vital aspect of your journey towards greatness – the art of celebrating your achievements along the way. Picture this: you're climbing a mountain, and with every step, you're getting closer to the peak. Now, what if you didn't stop to catch your breath, enjoy the view, and pat yourself on the back for how far you've come? That would be quite the missed opportunity, right? Well, the same goes for your path towards your goals.

Why Celebrate?

You might wonder, "Why bother celebrating the small wins when I'm focused on the big picture?" Well, think of celebrating as fuel for your drive engine. Acknowledging your successes, no matter how small, boosts your confidence, sparks your energy, and keeps your spirits high. It's like giving yourself a high-five and saying, "Hey, I'm doing awesome!"

The Ripple Effect

Celebrating isn't just about giving yourself a mini-party; it has a spread effect. When you enjoy your successes, you create a good loop. It boosts your mood and attitude, making you more eager to face the next task. Plus, it pushes those around you – friends, family, coworkers – to follow your lead and enjoy their own wins. Your happiness becomes contagious!

How to Celebrate Wisely

Now that we've established why celebrating is crucial, let's talk about how to do it right:

Set Milestones: Break down your bigger goals into smaller milestones. These could be finishing a part of your project, hitting an exercise goal, or even simply keeping a regular routine. Each time you hit a milestone, it's time for a party!

Be Playful: Celebrating doesn't have to be a grand event. It could be treating yourself to your favorite snack, dancing to your favorite song, or taking a moment to relax with a good book. Keep it light, fun, and individualized.

Reflect and Appreciate: Take a moment to reflect on your trip. Think about where you started and where you are now. Appreciate the work you've made. It's like looking at a "before and after" picture of your success story.

Share the Joy: Don't be shy to share your successes with your support system. Tell your friends, family, or workers about your latest achievement. Their cheers and applause will amplify your party.

pictorial Reminders: Create a pictorial picture of your successes. It could be a wall of sticky notes, a record of accomplishments, or even a computer Tracker. Seeing your progress clearly can be incredibly inspiring.

Practice Self-Compassion: Sometimes, despite your best efforts, you might fall short of a goal. It's okay! Celebrate the work you put in, the lessons you learned, and your drive to growth. Every step counts.

Remember, celebrating isn't about bragging or showing off – it's about praising your hard work and commitment. Your road towards success is a set of steps, and each step is a win in itself. So, go ahead, raise that imagined prize, do a little happy dance, and celebrate your amazing self. You deserve it!

Strategies for Maintaining Momentum and Avoiding Complacency

Congratulations on your journey as an Action Taker! By now, you've understood the amazing power of taking action and have achieved some remarkable goals. But how do you ensure that this fresh energy doesn't fizzle out, leaving you stuck in a rut of complacency? In this chapter, we'll dive into simple Yet effective strategies to keep that fire going and continue your journey of growth and achievement.

1. Set Progressive Goals: Keep the Target Moving

One key to continued energy is setting increasing goals. As you achieve one goal, quickly set your thoughts on the next one. This practice keeps you focused, involved, and always looking for growth. Each milestone you achieve becomes a stepping stone towards a bigger mission.

2. Break It Down: Small Steps, Big Impact

When keeping progress, break down your goals into smaller, doable steps. This avoids overload and gives a steady stream of awards. Remember, it's not about the size of the step, but the regularity of the action.

3. Reflect and Celebrate: Acknowledge Your Wins

Don't forget to stop and enjoy your successes along the way. Reflect on your trip and honor the progress you've made. Celebrating wins boosts your Confidence and fuels your drive to keep going forward.

4. Embrace Continuous Learning: Knowledge Is Fuel

Stay open and eager to learn. Seek out new skills, ideas, and views that can improve your trip.

Learning keeps your mind active, sparks imagination, and gives you with fresh tools to face obstacles.

5. Surround Yourself with Supportive People: Share the Journey

Connect with like-minded people who uplift and inspire you. Share your goals and success with friends, family, or a guide. Their support and thoughts can provide the extra push you need to stay on track.

6. Regularly Assess and Adjust: Stay Flexible

Periodically examine your goals and tactics. Are they still united with your vision? Are you facing new obstacles? Be open to changing your direction As needed. Flexibility ensures that you're always going in the right direction, even if the road changes.

7. Visualize Your Success: See It to Believe It

Use the power of imagination to keep your energy strong. Imagine yourself achieving your goals in vivid detail. Visualization not only boosts your confidence but also strengthens your resolve to action.

8. Stay Organized: Clutter-Free Mind, Clear Path

Maintain a tidy setting, both physically and online. Clutter can cause mental hurdles and slow down your progress. A clear and organized area promotes a clear and focused mind, ready to take on tasks.

9. Practice Self-Care: Fuel Your Body and Mind

Your well-being is important for keeping progress. Prioritize self-care through right diet, exercise, sleep, and rest. A healthy body and mind provide the energy and resiliency needed to keep going forward.

10. Share Your Journey: Inspire Others

As you keep your progress, share your journey with others. Your story of growth, failures, and successes can inspire and drive those around you. By being a light of action, you create a good spread effect in your community.

Remember, keeping progress is about consistency, commitment, and the unshakable confidence that you're capable of achieving greatness. By adopting these strategies, you'll continue to grow as an Action Taker, reaching new levels of success and satisfaction in every area of your life. Stay committed, keep taking action, and enjoy the amazing trip ahead!

Conclusion

As you reach the final pages of "Get Things Done: The Action Taker's Guide to Overcoming Excuses," take a moment to think on the amazing journey you've started upon. You've dug into the world of proactive attitude, beat delay, and harnessed the power of constant action. You've learned to turn excuses into moving stones and watched personally the deep effect of your resolve.

Remember, the road of an Action Taker is not a goal, but a lifelong journey. The tactics you've found in these chapters are not mere tools; they are the building blocks of a purpose-driven and happy life. Each step you take, each task you beat, and each goal you achieve pushes you further along this amazing road.

As you move forward, keep the light of drive burning brightly. Set your goals on new areas, break down obstacles, and continuously strive for growth. Embrace the power of responsibility, enjoy your wins, and stay open to change. The road may have its twists and turns, but armed with the knowledge and insights learned from this book, you have the tools to handle them with grace and resolve.
You are now prepared to inspire not only yourself but also those around you. Your journey as an Action Taker serves as a light of promise, telling others that reasons can be conquered, dreams can be achieved, and a life of meaningful action is within reach.

Thank you for starting on this changing journey with "Get Things Done." Now, it's time to accept your role as a powerful Action Taker, to make your mark on the world, and to shape your fate through the power of direct action. Your story is just beginning, and the pages ahead are waiting to be filled with your successes, your effect, and your unwavering commitment to getting things done. Onward, Action Taker, and may your journey be nothing short of amazing.